THE CIRCLE
OF WEALTH
51.4 DEGREES OF SUCCESS

LEE A. ARNOLD

I'M THE SOLUTION PUBLISHING

COEUR D ALENE, IDAHO

The Circle of Wealth
By Lee A Arnold

ISBN: 978-09817221-2-2
Library of Congress 2015945212

If you are offended by Christian or religious material and do not want to go further in this book, mail it back to me with the book's receipt at:

He's the Solution
701 E Front Ave.
Coeur d'Alene, ID 83814
I will give you a full retail refund including shipping. - Lee A. Arnold

Cover by River3.com

Printed and Digitized in the
United States of America

DEDICATION

God is first, family is second, and my career is third. Therefore, I first want to dedicate this book to my Lord and Savior Jesus Christ. Because of Him, I will spend an eternity in Heaven.

I also want to thank my Mom and Dad for raising me in a Christian home and teaching me the value of being born again.

To my wife Jaclyn for her constant and undying support of this entrepreneurial, crazy life. And to my kids for inspiring me to always be better, while reminding me the importance of a single minute of quality time with them.

I am also thankful for the realization that what we do on this earth has no bearing on the wealth we generate but rather the wealth we leave in the hearts and minds of people.

CONTENTS

INTRODUCTION

The idea for The Circle of Wealth first came to me while flying back from one of my three-day, real estate investment seminars in San Antonio. I was sitting beside a new employee, who I will call, "Brad." Brad was a very creative man in his mid-fifties, who I had just hired only a day or two before the event. Although he hardly knew me, I invited him to come along, hoping to give him a feel for the company. I figured that would be the fastest way to initiate him into what we do. To his credit, he agreed to come.

The plane got up to its cruising altitude and the seat belt sign went off. I sat back, turned to Brad and said, "So, what did you think of the seminar?"

He stared at me a minute, with a really sad look in his eyes, and then said, "Lee, I feel like a complete loser."

That just about took my breath away. At any of my events it has never been my aim to make anyone feel like a loser. That's not a message that I ever want to send. Although, I do try to give my students a healthy dose of financial reality, my goal is to inspire them and give them hope. I might be blunt, but I always want to throw them a life-line. I kind of coughed out, "What do you mean?"

Brad said, "I just realized I'm a screw up."

I really wanted to understand. "What do you mean?" I asked.

"I thought I was just coming to the seminar to, you know, get an intro-duction to you and the company. I didn't know what to expect. I didn't think I was going to get a revelation of how much I needed to rearrange my mental furniture where finances and success are concerned."

I had to think about that. Brad has an interesting way of expressing himself. "What do you mean?" I said, thinking that I was starting to sound like a broken record.

"I always thought things are just the way they are. You're either successful or you're not. I didn't even know I could move my furniture – mentally I mean. And I didn't know what it would look like if the furniture needed to be rearranged. I had no tangible frame of reference for thinking any way other than the way I always have. I'm getting close to sixty years old. I should be further along in my career. I should be saving for retirement. Actually I should have already saved for retirement. I should be doing something meaningful with my life."

My heart went out to him. I said, "So that's what you meant by 'I feel like a loser?'"

"Yes. It wasn't until you explained how someone sees things when their thinking needs to change that I realized you were painting a picture of me. I felt so stupid. Now I see that I've been letting life pass me by. It was hard to face, but I knew then that I had to get busy and make some real changes. For the sake of my family and myself."

"Sounds like you knew there was something you needed to know to be successful, but you didn't know what it was. You just needed someone who has been where you are to help you find it."

Brad nodded. "Exactly."

It was then that I began thinking about ways to help people like Brad see the financial picture they've been looking at all their lives, but never understood. It was also then that I began formulating my ideas about The Circle of Wealth.

Before I continue, let me say here that I believe in God. While this isn't a religious book, my faith plays a large role in my life, and throughout, I will emphasize some of my points with Biblical Scriptures. If that bothers you, this book may not be your cup of tea. If that's the case, I'll be happy to give you a refund. My contact information can be found in the back.

I believe that God is ultimately in control. I also believe that He has given each of us talents and opportunities. He places us in circumstances, situations and environments to bless us, teach us, or reach us and then gives us the opportunity to react. That reaction is probably the most important thing to understand about The Circle of Wealth.

DEFINING THE CIRCLE

So, what is The Circle of Wealth? In essence, The Circle of Wealth is a way of doing business. It's a meeting place for a closely-knit community of investors and producers of wealth. There's no membership fee or cost to join. All it takes to be involved is a simple decision that you want to part of it.

You may be wondering about the subtitle – 51.4 Degrees of Success. It's simple. There are seven parts to The Circle of Wealth, and 360 degrees in a circle. Dividing 360 by seven gives you 51.4. So, 51.4 Degrees of Success.

All you need to join The Circle is the willingness to learn and to serve by giving back what you've learned and earned.

Since the word "gospel" literally means "good news," you could say The Circle of Wealth is the gospel of business, commerce, and growth. In this book, I'm simply attempting to define the parameters by which this good news exists and how and why it works.

The Circle of Wealth has always existed within business networks as a network within a network. It's simply a referral system through which people say yay or nay to investing their time, money or talent in a specific person or an opportunity, based on the person's reputation and the value of the opportunity.

For example – say there is a group of doctors who play golf together on a regular basis. They all know and respect each other. As affluent people, they often talk about investments. Perhaps one has heard of a new start-up company that looks promising. He knows the founder and he's heard that investors are getting a 20% return. Maybe another heard from a trusted friend about a piece of real estate for sale that's about to be re-zoned to twice as many lots. Since the doctors know and respect one another, they can have confidence in sharing the quality of the investments with each other. They have a "Circle of Wealth."

♦ ♦ ♦

Because wealth is created by repeat business, an underlying premise of The Circle of Wealth is to remove the common, one-time transactional nature of most monetary relationships. Unlike the way transactional economics work, profit isn't the only motive in The Circle of Wealth. Instead, you want the best outcome for everyone involved in the transaction.

The idea isn't, "Thanks for the $20 and we're done." Or even worse, "Since I don't care whether I ever do business with you again, it doesn't matter how bad I screw you in this deal."

In a simple sense, the premise of The Circle of Wealth is more like, "Thanks for the $20. Now, how can we reinvest that $20 in what you're doing or what I'm doing so we can make more money together?" It's not just a one-time transaction, but rather a "You bless me and I bless you" type of relationship. We continue to benefit from each other. It's circular and never ending.

♦ ♦ ♦

Here's an important question to ask yourself before you enter The Circle of Wealth—"Why do I want to be wealthy?"

If you enter The Circle of Wealth only to make money, then The Circle is really no place for you. If you come with the idea that you just want to get rich quick, it would be preferable that you stay out. In fact, you can't join with the expectation only to take. You come in with the willingness to give, to lend, and to borrow. You borrow what you need and then you pay it back with interest. Those inside The Circle are there to give abundantly and bless everyone in all parts of The Circle. You'll find that you'll get more of what you want, by helping others get more of what they want.

Think of The Circle of Wealth as a library filled with finances and knowledge that you can borrow at will. Yet, you borrow with the understanding that you will bring back part of what you've gained, along with what you've borrowed.

What do I mean by that? You can come borrow what you need: mentoring, consulting, time, talent, and/or money, but here is no just taking. You're learning, earning, and borrowing because you understand that you will be able to give back of your time, talents, and money later on when you are in the position to do so.

You use what you need from The Circle now, knowing that you will not only pay back what you've borrowed, but also give back even more in the future. The result is a tangible reward for you, those you borrow from and those you will eventually give to.

Membership in The Circle mandates that when you achieve your goals, you will go back and help those who are just starting out and shepherd them through the process. You learn from those who are willing to teach, and then teach those who are willing to learn. To me, that's what The Circle of Wealth represents. You're not just building a portfolio of investments or a portfolio of properties, you're also building a portfolio of the people who you meet and work with along the way. If you build your business correctly, not only are you making money at all levels, you're also getting to know people who you can grow with and learn from.

That's the true value of The Circle of Wealth.

◆ ◆ ◆

When you borrow from The Circle of Wealth, you start by saying, "I want to _____" put what you want to do in the blank. "And I need _____" set the amount. "And I'll do it by _____" set the date. Once you have a deal, now you have an obligation to do something that's almost unheard of in business—keep the terms of the agreement. Then do it again, and again, and again.

If you do that, people in The Circle will begin to notice you. Because you've proven that you are a person of your word, they'll invite you to invest with them on a regular basis. Once you've hit this level, the returns are great and the upside is tremendous. It's called building reputational, as well as financial capital. You're building a reputation of being a performer and producer, and you're gaining wealth at the same time. If you succeed, everyone in The Circle will celebrate and applaud your success. If you don't, your reputational capital will suffer and you'll lose your momentum.

There is no room for people who only want to "try" in The Circle of Wealth. There is only room for those who "will." All the opportunity you could ask for exists within The Circle, but if you defraud, lie, cheat, steal or disappoint, you're out.

♦ ♦ ♦

I was talking about my ideas for this book with a business associate and she asked, "Lee, what happens if a person doesn't even know there is a Circle of Wealth? Does it still work for them?"

My reply, "The Circle of Wealth is in operation whether you're aware of it or not. Just because you aren't aware of something doesn't mean it doesn't exist. It only means that you may not be reaping any of the rewards."

She said, "Okay. Then can you fail in The Circle?" "Yes. Failure is possible. But not for the reasons you might think. And not for the usual reasons that hold people back."

If you're not going to do what it takes to produce or you're not going to give back there is no place for you in The Circle. If you don't fulfill your promises, or you defraud people, or you misrepresent yourself, again, you're out. Simple as that.

What a shame to have everything it takes to succeed, without the moral character to sustain success. It's tragic.

♦ ♦ ♦

Your opportunity to enter The Circle began by buying this book. You might say, "Well, if that's all it takes to start, how come everyone isn't living in The Circle of Wealth?"

Good question. Here's a scenario that will illustrate the answer. I like to think big, so let's say 1 million people buy this book. Then, based on a rough publishing industry estimate, let's say only a quarter of them finish reading it. Actually, it's less than that, but I like to be optimistic. Then, let's say a mere 10% of those who read the book apply any of what they have learned from it. That eliminates a whopping 975,000 potential candidates from The Circle. That's 975,000 people who haven't even come up to the starting gate, let alone run the race.

I would bet most of our 975,000 potential Circle members don't have much, if any, savings. Most of them are probably living paycheck to paycheck at a dead-end job.

You may say, "Yeah, but your book can't be the only way into The Circle of Wealth. Maybe they'll find another way."

Maybe. But if I was going to bet, I would bet that if they don't bother to read or implement the information in a book they've already paid good money for and they already have in their possession, they most likely won't implement any other strategy for success either.

That said, I must confess there are business books on my shelf that I haven't finished reading yet, or haven't even started. However, in my defense, I'm too busy implementing what I've learned in all the other books I've already read. At the same time, there are many books that I've already read two or three times, made notes in and dog-eared the pages so I can refer back to them time and time again.

Now let's create an imaginary Circle of Wealth candidate who has read the book and decided to implement the information. We'll call him "Tom." Let's say Tom is highly motivated and he wants to be a real estate investor. In the five years since he bought the book, Tom has come to four of my trainings, borrowed over $1 million from my company to buy properties, which he's sold, and now he's reinvesting his profits into two loans for other motivated real estate investors who are now paying him interest. He's increased his savings to $600,000. If I come across a deal that requires multiple investors, guess who I'll call? Tom.

In The Circle of Wealth, I can learn from those who have gone before me. I have access to expert help, counselors, mentors, and advisors.

Proverbs 15:22

> *Plans fail for lack of counsel, but with many advisers they succeed.* (NIV)

You may be thinking, "Well, I'd like to join The Circle of Wealth, but I have nothing to give. I don't have any money. I don't have a degree. I don't have great credit."

All that may be true. It was true for me at one time too, but in The Circle of Wealth none of that matters. I joined by finding an opportunity, which I used to enter The Circle of Wealth. This opportunity is what attracted someone else in The Circle who saw potential and believed in me enough to invest with me. Since then, I have continued my journey in The Circle of Wealth as both the borrower and lender, but it was that first deal that was instrumental to my successful beginning.

Many beginning entrepreneurs make the mistake of thinking they don't bring anything to the table and that they're beholden to the lender. There could be nothing further from the truth. The person with money needs an opportunity to make a return on an investment and the person who needs money provides that opportunity. That's a foundational principle of The Circle.

If you don't have financial capital, you come to The Circle of Wealth with your opportunity and you give people who have money the ability to make a return on their investment in you and your opportunity.

Why would a perfect stranger want to invest in your opportunity? Money sitting in a bank savings account currently earns 1 to 2% interest. A mutual fund or money market account makes close to 3%, if you're lucky. Money in the bond market gets killed by inflation. So bringing someone an opportunity to make 7 to 12% on a secured real estate loan, for example, is an amazing gift. So my question is, who is actually helping who here?

That's how a person in Part 1 of The Circle gives. You give people, who have money to invest, something worthwhile to invest in. The idea isn't, "I'm borrowing $75,000, so I'm just taking from The Circle." No. The Circle of Wealth doesn't work that way. You're creating investment opportunities for others. The service you perform when you are in Part 1 is vitally important to The Circle of Wealth's well-being.

All Parts of The Circle need all the other parts to work properly. True, a borrower needs someone with money to borrow from, but a person with money needs a borrower with the drive, skill-set, and ability to give them a return on their investment.

In my own business, I'm often in the position of sitting on money that I'd like to invest. My need and desire is to find someone who will bring me a great deal that I can invest in.

If you're in the first parts of The Circle, you may have no higher education that can be translated into a trade or business. You may have no money to invest and no knowledge of how to start a business. But, be encouraged, there are some in The Circle who have started with even less than you, but have made the effort to get an education and gain experience. They may have done some investing and have a few deals under their belt. They now have some financial wherewithal – between $10,000 to $50,000 in the bank – and they now can partner with others in The Circle on investments.

You simply begin where you are and to do that, you just need to make the decision to get started and then start.

A person who has gone through The Circle has learned how to gather wealth. I made my fortune in real estate, so a lot of my examples come from that field. However The Circle of Wealth isn't only about real estate. It can work in any industry. The great thing is, if you've learned how to excel in one industry, you can apply that knowledge to any business, in any location, at any time. Who knows? You could go out to your garage and develop the next big thing. Then you just bring that opportunity to someone in The Circle for advice, marketing, and funding. The rules don't change. It's the same game every time.

People often try to either skip or speed through the first parts of The Circle. They try to skip the hard work that needs to be done in taking inventory of their strengths and weaknesses. Why? Because the first parts aren't fun. In fact, sometimes they are pretty painful, but if you're scraping your knees, trust me, you're moving forward and you're learning something.

If you don't go through the process though, you'll never know what your weaknesses are or where your thinking is skewed. Many entrepreneurs are like that– they want to skip the homework and just take the test. I'm guilty of that too.

The CEO of LinkedIn once said that an entrepreneur is like someone who jumps off a cliff and tries to figure out how to make a parachute on the way down. That pretty much sums it up. The longer I've been at this, the more I appreciate taking the time to do my homework. The times I've fallen the hardest were the times when I rushed through the planning process.

Every degree you achieve in The Circle gives you knowledge and credibility that makes you even more valuable in the marketplace. However, if you haven't learned the steps by going through all the parts of The Circle of Wealth, I doubt you'll be as successful as you could be if you had.

I once heard a wise saying: shirtsleeves to shirtsleeves in three generations. "Shirtsleeves" refers to blue-collar workers. The principle plays out like this – immigrant parents come to this country and work their tail off. Their children watch as they gather a modest fortune and are then able to put their children through college and eventually pass on the family business and a small fortune. The children take the experience and lessons of their parents and do even better financially. However, when the children have their own children, they often spoil them. They give them all the worldly possessions they never had growing up without any emphasis on the hard work it takes to earn them. Their children never understand the value of money and are only interested in spending it. They blow through the family fortune and eventually end up back where the family initially started, thus the term shirtsleeves to shirtsleeves in three generations.

Becoming part of The Circle is the greatest opportunity that will ever come your way. People who thrive within The Circle are aggressive, motivated, and willing to mentor, help, and give back. If you apply what you learn from this book, it can start you on the path to a better life.

You probably have a dream, vision, or desire. Otherwise, you wouldn't be reading this book. It was written for those who want to make the choice to follow their dreams. It's my hope that when you've read it, you'll see where you are within The Circle and it will help you to understand how to use its power to gain greater success.

After reading, you may choose to move forward and venture out or you may put the book down and choose to do nothing. In the end it's your choice. My goal, whatever part of The Circle you're in, is to encourage you to become so enthusiastic and passionate that you go out and make something happen – for yourself and also for someone else.

The first steps in The Circle aren't easy, but if you're not hard on yourself, life will be. So, here we go.

PART 1
AWARENESS

Having dreams and goals accelerates the acquisition of wealth, and the acquisition of wealth accelerates the fulfillment of dreams. It's circular, and it's a foundational principle of The Circle of Wealth.

It's good to have money for the good it can do, but the point of life isn't to just gain material wealth. The point of life is to live and live well. So the real question is, how well will you live? Regardless of who you are, or where you've been, you can become who and what you want to be. Successful people aren't born that way. They become successful by what they believe and the choices they make. All people possess the potential for greatness. The question is whether or not they will choose to use their potential.

The famous phrase by Thomas Edison, "Genius is one percent inspiration and ninety-nine percent perspiration," is an exact and honest statement. Another quote of his, "The chief ingredients for success are imagination, plus ambition and the will to work," is just as accurate.

The idea that people are either talented or they're not results in all sorts of misguided notions. While a person may have talent in some area, there's no guarantee that they will ever accomplish anything meaningful with that talent. They may be really nice people, with lots of potential, yet never do much with it. Even amazingly talented people won't attain success if they aren't motivated to action.

Accomplishment has a whole work-flow associated with it according to Thomas Edison. "Work" is the key word. Just as important are initiative, motivation, and perseverance. Anyone, gifted or not, can use them to achieve a goal. So, in reality, the potential for greatness is only measured by how far a person decides to go.

You may have heard of, or know, someone who seems to have an amazing financial touch. Everything they get involved with makes money. Do they have a gift? Are they special? Or are they just lucky? While I can't say with certainty that no one has ever had a special gift for making money, I wouldn't bet on it.

In my experience, the special gift is hard work.

Some people may think I'm lucky because I have a nice house, a nanny, a lawn service, etc. The truth is, I'm not lucky. I've made some really hard decisions about what I wanted my life to look like and I wasn't willing to bend. Those who say I'm lucky haven't seen me going to the airport at 4:00 AM to catch a plane, working eighteen-hour days, being away from my family on a regular basis, or putting my livelihood on the line by taking on a new investment. I'm not lucky. I'm hard-working and extremely motivated. There's a big difference.

◆ ◆ ◆

Why does one person succeed when another fails? It's an often-asked question. It sometimes seems that it's up to some mystical, magical act of fate, but there is a straightforward explanation.

Almost everyone has an exceptional dream and expectation for their life. They feel the intense magic and excitement whenever they think about it. Yet many people don't take the necessary action and steps to put that dream into motion. Instead they allow time to trample their dream. Then one day, years later, they wake up and find themselves in the same position they were in when they first had the dream and they wonder, "How did this happen? Why did I never follow through on this or that great idea?"

So what was it that happened? Nothing. Nothing happened. They took no initiative. They took no action. Even though they knew what they wanted to do, they really never had the intention of actually doing it. To achieve a goal, the desire for the goal must be combined with both initiative and action. It's a simple as that.

Who you are and where you've been isn't what prevents you from becoming who you want to be. Though a lot of people think that. It's the lack of action that prevents you from going forward. That, and a lack motivation – the thing that gets you going on a project and keeps you going until you finish it.

So, the first step to achieving a dream is to take action.

Making choices without taking action is useless. A positive choice should immediately be followed by a positive action. Whatever the goal is, the mantra should be, "Get busy doing it!"

It has been said, "If it was easy, everyone would do it." That phrase has been used about all sorts of subjects, but regardless the concept is absolutely true. The more difficult something is, the fewer the people will try to tackle it.

♦ ♦ ♦

Basically, the law of cause and effect says that any action will have a result. It's a law of physics and it's a fundamental truth. Whether we know what the cause is, or whether we see the effect, there is always a cause to every effect. When making choices, try to determine what causes are creating what effects in your life.

Past choices influence present choices. Present choices influence future choices. A pattern begins taking shape with each choice you make and this is how habits are formed, both good and bad.

Without a strong desire to make a change, a person's choices will fall into a well-worn pattern – positive or negative. To change your life though, you'll have to change your habits. It's not easy to change a habit, and as I said before if it were easy, everyone would be doing it.

The key is to put more energy into actions that produce positive results rather than those that produce negative outcomes. Once you've learned how to acquire positive traits, you can also learn how to spur yourself into action.

All the progress that has ever been made by anyone, in any field, has been made by those who took action. If you want to achieve something, do something to achieve it. It's by taking action that a dream becomes a reality.

Now here's the part nobody is crazy about – changing habits and taking action is work and often it's W.O.R.K. However, that's what it takes to achieve your goals, so therefore the choice is quite simple – **JUST DO IT.**

It's pretty obvious that there's hard work involved in success. Almost every self-help book and anyone who is successful will tell you that. However, what may be an absolute shocker to you is that it's actually easier to succeed than it is to fail. It may not seem like it at the outset, but it's true. There is a lot of hard work that goes into failing. The hard work of failing, or choosing not to succeed, comes in the form of despair, hopelessness, and depression.

◆ ◆ ◆

You shape and construct your life from the inside out. Your attitudes, your customs, and your beliefs are what you build it with. Perhaps you've built a structure with doors and windows that are open to knowledge and new ideas. Maybe you've built walls that prevent anything new from entering. Success or failure are mainly determined by the materials, energy, and time you devote to the project.

You are a product of your family, your relationships, and your environment. That being the case, you're also the absolute ruler of what you think, feel, and believe. You ultimately control your destiny. A thought is the most persuasive form of suggestion. They are the most powerful building blocks available to human beings. They are more powerful than anything you perceive with your five physical senses – vision, hearing, smell, taste, touch.

By controlling your thoughts, you can control your emotions. But when thoughts alone can't stop your negative emotions, sometimes taking positive action will.

The ability to control your thoughts is possibly the greatest asset a person can possess. If you can learn to keep your focus on what you want in your life, and off what you don't want, you will move farther and faster on the road to success.

It's been said that the only way to change a thought is to speak words. So if your thoughts are straying into negative territory, the fastest way to turn them around is to say something positive out loud. Even if you only say it to yourself. Whenever I'm aware that my mood is flying south, I say something positive and pretty soon, I realize that my attitude has changed for the better.

You can put positive sayings all over the place. Tape them to your bathroom mirror, hang them on the refrigerator, put them on your desk, or even in your car. A positive attitude will go a long way in helping you on your journey. It will help you believe in your abilities, find the strength to keep going when you feel like quitting, and allow you to weather the storms in your life. However, if you wait, once you're in the middle of a crisis, if you aren't already in the habit of thinking positively, it's almost impossible to learn.

Overcoming adversity makes a strong person stronger. It's a blessing in disguise. Remember this, along with most disadvantages comes an advantage. It may be well-hidden, but it's there. You just have to look for it.

◆ ◆ ◆

Everyone has opportunities available to them. But rather than accept responsibility for their lives, some people prefer to believe that they have no control over the hand that life has dealt them.

It's important to take responsibility for your life. Admit that if you aren't where you want to be, it's your own fault. You need to eliminate all excuses. In fact, I would encourage you to not allow yourself even one. Just get rid of all of them. Don't allow yourself to think, or don't allow others to tell you, that it's okay, you can't help it, or it's not your fault. Realize there is really no excuse, no reason not to do it, and ultimately that you have everything to lose and nothing to gain when you fall back on your excuses.

Questions to ask yourself, "Have I been making excuses for not going after my dreams? Have I really been trying? Have I put the blame on others when I should have put it on myself?"

The next step will be to overcome any circumstance that even looks like an obstacle. Overcoming circumstances begins by not accepting that your current position as permanent. One of my favorite business books was written way back in 1962. In *The Success System That Never Fails*, author William Clement Stone says:

> *"Every man, every successful man, no matter what the field of endeavor, has known the magic of these words: Every adversity has the seed of an equivalent or greater benefit."*

What he's saying is, whenever you come across an obstacle on your road to success, the wisest thing you can do is to see it as a blessing in disguise. I can tell you from personal experience that it's true. What you learn by overcoming an obstacle will far and away make up for any aggravation it causes.

◆ ◆ ◆

Poor people perpetually say, "I can't." Rich people habitually say, "How can I?"

The Circle of Wealth offers a compass to help you on the journey from someone who consistently says, "I can't," to someone who steadfastly says, "How can I?"

It's been said that what the mind can conceive and believe, the mind can achieve. Because, if you think you can't, then you really can't. But if you believe that you can, then you really do have a shot at it. Even saying the word "believe" when I'm thinking about something I want to do, makes me feel more like I can do it.

Let's say you want to move to a better neighborhood. The new house will cost $1,500 a month and you're currently only paying $800, which means you have a $700 a month difference. A person who is bound by circumstances will say, "I can't afford that." However a person who is serious about overcoming their circumstances will say, "How can I make an extra $700 a month?"

That person will start doing the math. If they make $10 an hour, in order to make the extra $700, they will need to work seventy additional hours a month. Divide that into four weeks – 17 ½ extra hours. Divide that into five workdays – 3 ½ hours a day, which is something a motivated person could do.

I can almost hear the unmotivated people now. "But, Lee, I'm busy. I can't work an extra seventy hours a month." Right away, they're reacting to the largest, most daunting number of hours, instead of breaking it down into small enough increments that it looks feasible. The motivated people will take it even farther. They'll start thinking of ways they can make more per hour, so they won't need to work as many hours.

♦ ♦ ♦

Another key to overcoming an obstacle is to identify a clear reason why you want to overcome it. What is the reason or reasons? If you don't have a clear idea why you want to go from A to B, then you'll most likely, when the road gets rough, be waylaid somewhere on the journey.

Why do you want to be successful? The answer to that question could be anything as long as it truly motivates you toward success. For example, your children or spouse could be great motivators. Even if people aren't motivated to move forward by their own desires, they are often motivated by the desire to make life better for their families.

♦ ♦ ♦

In a financial transaction the money flows back and forth. And you're either on one side of the equation or the other. On one side you're handing over your money, and on the other side you're shoving the money in your pocket. To be wealthy, you have to learn how to shove a lot more money in your pocket than you hand over.

There are also two parties in any economic transaction – producers and consumers. Everyone buys something and everyone sells something – even if what we sell is our time to an employer. If you had the proverbial lemonade stand, you've gone from being a consumer to being a producer.

To be successful, either you need to be a producer of something that a whole lot of people will pay a small amount for, or a producer of something a few people will pay a whole lot for.

In The Circle of Wealth, you could argue that borrowers and lenders are both producers and consumers. Those who borrow consume what the lenders lend. But you could also argue that borrowers are producers because lenders consume the deals they bring to the table. Again, it's circular. Neither one has a clear advantage.

♦ ♦ ♦

I believe we're obligated to use our God-given talents to learn to take care of ourselves, and then to bless others. America was founded by people who were sick and tired of having someone else running their lives. However, what we see now, to a large degree, is too much dependence on government, big business, and employers.

Dependence on government doesn't work, and has never worked in the history of mankind. Taxing the rich so the government can distribute it to the poor under the guise that it's helping may sound good, but that model is flawed at its core. It's been proven by history to be flawed. It doesn't work. Wealthy people begin to think, "Why on earth am I working my tail off? If the government is just going to take what I earn and give it to someone who isn't working, why should I bother?"

Powerful institutions know that if the populace is dependent, then in a sense those institutions can do whatever they want. They don't offer any way for the average man – who has less than perfect credit, less than perfect payment history, or less than perfect bank accounts – access to the American Dream. What this does is habituate the usual way of thinking that if big government, big business, big banks, or your employer won't help you get ahead, then you're stuck.

The government tracks the creation of jobs. It's a major economic indicator. But why don't they keep statistics on the creation of new companies? Why don't they track new entrepreneurs, or new investment opportunities in the same way? I don't know the answer to that question. It looks to me like the government isn't really interested in your independence.

That said, it's more beneficial for everyone concerned to allow the rich to be rich, and for the poor to learn by their example, how to become rich.

When I was the guy with a low-paying job and thought I had no real opportunity, I wish someone would have told me I had significant value. I wish I would have been told about The Circle of Wealth and how I could bring opportunity to people with far more money than I had, and thereby work and earn a good living.

I think we, as a society, don't look at people in the right light or understand their talents. Take panhandlers, for example. Some could be employed as copywriters. I heard of a guy who had eight different signs. He would market-test each one to figure out which one worked the best in the morning commute traffic, which one worked better for midday, and which one worked best for the evening rush hour. He honed it down to a science. He actually knew which sign would outperform another and by what percentage. Eventually he learned so much about marketing, that he became a marketing consultant.

Only in America, right?!

♦ ♦ ♦

Why should you care about any of this? If you don't understand these principles and create a plan for your life, life will have a plan for you. When I was younger, I didn't have any notion of what I wanted to do with my life, but my parents did. Their plan was for me to graduate from high school, go to college to get a degree, find a decent job, get married and have children, and work for thirty years and retire.

However that plan didn't work for me. From an early age I refused to allow someone else to control the way I think and act. I was fine with the get married and have children part of it, but the rest of it just didn't fit me.

First, I don't like participating in the conventional education model. I'm not the kind of person who does well being told what to do and when to do it. That's also why I couldn't clock in and out at the same company for thirty years with the ultimate desire of retiring and becoming idle one day. If someone wanted me to die a slow agonizing death, they could just put me in a job, with an hourly wage, and no opportunity for increase or advancement.

For many people, my parent's plan for me looks familiar. No offense to the parents out there, but it doesn't offer much in the way of hope, inspiration, or success. It's mundane, monotonous, and mediocre.

For one thing, most people haven't actually chosen to do what they're doing for a living. They're doing what they do by default. Here's how it usually goes. A person gets a job and they work at it awhile and then, before they know it, they're married, buying a house, and having children. By now, in their minds they're trapped and they can't change the equation.

If you haven't created another plan, this is most likely the pattern your life will also follow.

People often get stuck in that rut thinking, "This is what I've always done, so this is what I'm always going to do." They allow the idea of making a big change, like becoming an entrepreneur, being self-employed, or starting a business overwhelm them to the point that they stop in their tracks.

It's kind of like a car. If the wheels are in proper alignment and the road is level, when you let go of the steering wheel, by default, the car will go straight ahead until it runs out of gas. That's pretty much what happens when you follow the well-worn plan. You go until you run out of gas.

♦ ♦ ♦

Life is a ticking time bomb and death is final.

When people are nearing retirement, oftentimes there is a sudden awareness of the time that has passed. There is an acute comparison of where they wanted to be at that point in their lives to where they actually are and a painful understanding of all the missed opportunities and unfulfilled dreams.

This is how I am on vacation. The first two or three days, I'm pretty much immobile because I'm exhausted. Then, on day four I get my energy back and I try to cram everything I can into the last day or two of my vacation.

Life can be like me on vacation – laying around the first few days, then going hog-wild at the end. Many of us spend our formative years trying to avoid instruction and education. We spend our productive working years in the pursuit of recreation and relaxation. Then, at the time in our lives when we should be enjoying the fruits of our labor, we suddenly realize that there isn't any fruit. We've spent our entire lives avoiding labor—at least in a dynamic money-making sense. If we have labored, we find that the fruit is less than abundant and we find ourselves trying to cram it all in at the last minute.

We should always be growing and progressing from the time we're born to the time we die.

Here's another example. Let's say you have a two year-old child. Everything seems fine, but eventually you realize that all the other children are walking better, talking better, growing bigger, and learning faster than your son or daughter. If you're like me, it wouldn't take long for you to get your youngster to a doctor. You take immediate action because you know something is wrong with your child's progress and development. But in adults, we're often okay with some state of arrested life-development. We're used to seeing it in ourselves or others that we don't question why someone stays in some dead-end job. We don't go to a "self-help doctor" when we're trapped in a hamster-wheel existence and say, "My growth is stunted and I'm not where I want to be or I'm supposed to be. I need help."

The prescription for stunted financial development is multi-faceted and varies from person to person. A few suggestions: identify where you want to be financially. Read self-help books. Consult with an advisor. Go to motivational and educational seminars. Network with people who are where you want to be financially. However, the best solution is really to just **DO SOMETHING!**

Over the course of your life, you've probably experienced people and circumstances that have tried to hold you back. Now it's time learn to recognize who and what they are, and start actively avoiding them, especially the people. Negative people can have a profound influence over us, particularly those who are close to us like friends and family. Oftentimes, while they may appear to have your best interest at heart, they may actually be playing out their own fears and failures on the backdrop of your life.

Nothing could be more irrational than allowing another person's fear to hold you back. In order to move forward, you'll either have to develop a backbone or distance yourself from those who can influence you to compromise your goals and aspirations. Of the two, developing a backbone is the best choice. It will be invaluable to you, as you pursue your goals, to be able to stand your ground no matter what other people say. In fact, I don't think you'll actually be able to reach a meaningful goal without that ability, because no matter how hard you try, you can't continually run away from confrontation. Take it from me, at some point it will be necessary to face a conflict head on. So you might as well develop that backbone now. That's not to say you have to turn into a confrontational jerk. Just don't allow people to force you into a box and don't allow them to map out your boundaries for you.

Here's an illustration: let's say you hate cold weather, but live where there are really harsh winters. You want to move to Florida. The first hurdle you may face is, "I can't leave my job."

Really? Are you telling me that there are absolutely no jobs in Florida and that no one works in Florida? The truth is, your perception is telling you something like – you can't move because you might not find another job and if you do, it won't be as good as the one you have now. Because you believed this perception, not matter how false it may be, you choose to stay where you are.

The next hurdle might be, "I can't leave my family." Okay, fair enough. Family is important, but did you even ask them about it? Maybe they would welcome moving south too. Unless you entertain the idea and do the due diligence to see if your perceptions are right or wrong, you'll never know and you'll remain stuck wondering, "What if?"

The interesting thing about a road is that it leads two opposite directions. A road can either take you closer to your goal and your desired future or further away from it. For example, several years ago I chose to leave Salt Lake City for Spokane, Washington because I wanted to raise my family here. It was scary to relocate, knowing I would be displacing my business, opening up shop in a new market, and hiring all new people, but because I knew my family would do better in this environment, I took the risk. By doing what was best for my family, I've been more successful here than I was in Salt Lake City. The motivation reaped the reward.

The point is to understand how your perception of things influences your choices so you can start making choices that are more in line with the direction that you want your life to go.

Here's another thing that trips people up: "My spouse isn't happy about the changes I want to make."

This one can be hard to deal with. For better or worse, in most cases a person's spouse has more influence over them than anyone else. Don't move forward with major changes until your spouse is on board. That said, also remember that the key to having success in business and life is really all about sales. Getting your spouse on the same page with you is sale number one. You may need to dust off your sales techniques, but if you truly believe that the direction you want to go will be beneficial to you, your marriage, and your family, then do whatever it takes to get your spouse to believe it too. You made your spouse believe in you once, make it your aim to do it again. After all, he or she loved you enough to be sold on the idea of marrying you in the first place!

◆ ◆ ◆

Before you set out on your journey, it's important to discover your gifts and talents or your strengths and weaknesses. In my opinion, talent is a combination of two things: the thing you're best at and the thing you enjoy the most. When I'm consulting with someone, I try to ferret out their core competencies. I often ask, "If America suddenly became a communist nation and you had to choose to do one thing for a living for the rest of your life, knowing you couldn't change your mind later on and knowing you would get paid next to nothing, what would you do? What would you do for the rest of your life simply because you wanted to do it?"

That question takes the focus off the profit motive and puts it solidly on what the person wants to do and is actually good at.

In the next section we'll concentrate on gaining an understanding of who you are, what you're good at, and what you're not so good at. You'll need to know this so you can decide what you can do yourself and what you should have someone else to do. We'll also cover what has tripped you up and what has propelled you forward. I call it "Taking Inventory."

Some have said that Taking Inventory is the hardest part. It's true because it's not fun thinking about past failures and missed opportunities. However, the knowledge you gain by looking truthfully at your strengths and weaknesses will be invaluable to you on your road to success.

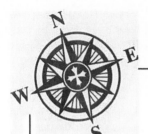

51.4 Degrees of

Awareness

1. Come to grips with unfulfilled dreams & goals.
2. Face the truth about why you haven't achieved your dreams.
3. Gain awareness of where you are in life.
4. Gain awareness of the way the financial world operates.
5. Face up to what it will take to achieve your goals.

TO ENHANCE YOUR FINANCIAL SUCCESS, WRITE DOWN FOCUSED GOALS THAT YOU WANT TO ACCOMPLISH THIS YEAR, 3 YEARS FROM NOW, AND FIVE YEARS FROM NOW.

_____

_____

_____

_____

_____

_____

_____

_____

_____

_____

PART 2
MY VENTURE

I had an idyllic childhood. I grew up on five acres on a bluff about fifteen minutes from downtown Spokane. Our property was on a dirt road that ran through a prairie surrounded by acres of wheat and alfalfa. Although we didn't have a large farm, we grew enough crops to sustain my family and make a profit.

My family was very traditional with my mother staying home to raise and care for me and my sisters while my father went to work. Although we weren't poor, my parents made sure to instill in us work ethic and therefore we had to earn money to buy our own school clothes, as well as anything else we wanted. It wasn't that my parents were unwilling to give us money, but that they wanted us to learn, first hand, how to work hard and to be self-sufficient.

The property where we lived consisted of a house, a barn, and a lawn that seemed like it took forever to mow. When I was around seven or eight, my father planted an acre and a half of strawberries and three acres of alfalfa. Each row of strawberries was about a thousand feet long. My parents paid me and my sisters $1 to weed a row. In the summer, my mother would wake us up early before it got too hot and after about three hours of weeding, I made one dollar. Although I didn't earn very much, I did learn the valuable lesson that if I wanted to make money I had to work.

Once I figured that out, I wanted to make more money. But because weeding strawberries was only a summertime business, I asked a man, who lived up the road and raised horses, if I could come work for him too. He paid me $1 per cleaned stall. So, every day after school I mucked out all eight of his stalls, which consisted of taking out and putting in fresh woodchips, and I made $8 a day. Not bad for an eight year-old.

One summer my parents decided to allow people to come and pick their own strawberries, which was fine with me because I was tired of picking them. My father put a sign out on the road that read "U-Pick Strawberries." This was the first time I understood the value of marketing. Neighbors and people driving by would stop to pick strawberries. We would give them a bucket to fill and then they would come up to the barn where my dad set up a long counter with a scale. The customers would bring back their bucket and we would weigh it, give them the price, and then we would package what they picked. I made $1,300 that summer, which was much better than weeding strawberries for a dollar a row or mucking out horse stalls for a dollar a stall.

I remember thinking, "This is cool. We took dirt, planted a crop and we created dollars and cents out of it." The problem with that business model is that you only get paid sixty days out of the year.

So I figured out other ways to earn money. I began mowing a neighbor's yard and they paid me $30 a week for a three-acre lot. About that same time, my father scrapped the strawberries and planted alfalfa. My grandmother bought five acres next to our property and also planted alfalfa and the farmer behind us planted alfalfa. In total, there were about eighteen acres of alfalfa. My father had a tractor, a cutter, and baler, so we cut the alfalfa, laid it out to dry, raked it, baled it, and then put it in the barn.

I put half of the alfalfa in my father's barn and the other half in neighbor's barn. When that was done, I helped the other neighboring farmers put up their hay too. I made $10 to $14 an hour baling hay that summer, which was also better than weeding strawberries and mucking horse stalls.

As I have found over the years, farming is no different than any other business. It is referral based. If you did a good job for one person, pretty soon everyone on the bluff was calling and you had plenty of work. I would wake up at 6:00 AM and ride my bike 10-20 miles to bale hay.

Although I was a small kid – a late bloomer – I could still outwork many of the other guys, usually football players, who were hired for the summer too. Even though they were bigger than me, I understood work ethic and could throw hay for ten hours, which was often much longer than many of them could. I would then ride my bike back home and do it all over again the next day – all summer long.

My grandfather on my mother's side was a fulltime rancher. He had a property with about a mile of riverfront on the St. Joe River in St. Maries, Idaho. When I was a little older I spent most summers there, working on the ranch. At the time, I didn't realize how special his land was.

Part of the property was shaded by a mountain and the other part was in the sun all day. In the sunny section, my grandfather grew alfalfa. In the shady section he had a huge barn where he kept about a hundred head of cattle. My cousins and I would help him put up his hay and slaughter the cows every year.

When you worked on the farm, you always started work about 6:00 AM and stopped at 11:30 AM. Then there was always a big lunch with roast beef, mashed potatoes and gravy, corn on the cob, freshly-squeezed lemonade – the works. I remember sitting at their dining table, looking out at that beautiful, serene river and watching the tugboats pulling logs down to the processing center while we ate.

After lunch my grandfather would take a nap and my cousins and I would go swimming. Sometimes we would ride the logs down the river to the mill.

I would also help my grandfather take cattle to auction at the Spokane Stockyard, which was about a two-hour drive from his ranch. We would load up in his big one-ton dually truck and a trailer which held eight cows. It was my first exposure to commerce and the marketplace. I recall the gleam in his eye when the cattle were led into the ring. He'd always say, "Okay, Lee, here we go!" Then the auction would begin and the whole place would turn electric as the auctioneer started calling out bids. The bidding began at $300 or $400 and every time a blue paddle went up, the price would increase by $50. I watched my grandfather make $4,000 in one day. That's 4,000 rows of strawberries weeded, 4,000 stalls mucked, or 400 hours baling hay!

I knew opportunity when I saw it. I thought, "I want to make money like that by raising my own cow." My grandfather said I could buy a calf at the auction for about $400 and sell it for $1,600 – that would be a 400% return on investment, if you didn't count the cost of feed. I didn't understand the nature of yield at that time, but I knew it was a good return. So I told my parents about my money-making venture and how I would need my dad to build me a fence.

My father never got around to building the fence and I never got around to buying the calf, but that summer taught me many important lessons about hard work and earning money on my own terms. Though my beginnings may have been ordinary enough, much of what I learned then has followed me throughout my career today. Learning the value of money and how to work hard have been defining points in my life. The lessons I learned then have been invaluable to me today.

PART 1
TAKING INVENTORY

When I go about fixing an investment house, the first thing I do is start ripping everything out. I just tear into it. Out goes the kitchen. Out goes the bathroom. Out goes the flooring. Out goes the wallpaper. It's hard to add new walls and paint if you still have all the old stuff in there. If there's anything of value that I want to keep, I can always put it back in.

After I get everything out of the house, then I can begin to get a picture of what I want to create. I know where I need to just do small fix ups and repairs and where I need to build from the ground up. I start formulating a plan of the materials I'll need to buy and the budget I'll need to get the job done. I make a list, take it to the home improvement center, and buy everything I need. Once I put everything where it needs to go, the property is transformed into something entirely different and it's much better than it was the day I found it. It's a home that is safe, comfortable, and beautiful – a place anyone would want to raise their family.

It's the same with people's thinking. If you're not where you want to be in your life, the fix starts by recognizing that you have a dirty, broken-down house and you need to tear out your old way of thinking to upgrade it.

You just need to rip the whole thing out. If there's something of value, you'll know it when you see it. Regardless, you need to take a hard look at everything – the way you think, the way you act, the way you react, the choices you make and fail to make, the things you're good at and the things you're bad at, the things you're scared of and the things you're not worried about at all. All of these factors make a difference to your success in life.

Some people think that by taking inventory they'll limit their options. Nothing could be further from the truth. What you are doing is throwing open the doors to more possibilities and opportunities by knowing what you're capable of and what you will need help with.

I heard a great saying once that went something like this: be proud of who you are and be the best you that you can be, because everyone else is already taken. There's only one you, so get busy being a great version of you. That's what you'll be doing in this Taking Inventory section. You'll find out who you are and who you're not. Once you know this, you can start on the journey to becoming the best version of who you want to be.

First ask yourself, "Am I who I want to be? Am I where I want to be?"

You should know what your strengths are. You should also know what your weaknesses are. You should know your abilities and your potential for growth. It is time to get a true picture of your financial outlook. Are you living paycheck to paycheck? Are you living beyond your means? Are your credit cards maxed-out? Are you paying your bills on time? It's time to reconcile yourself to the answers to those questions and then finally begin to do something about it!

♦ ♦ ♦

In Taking Inventory, you are learning to recognize the necessary ingredients for success. You will learn how to recognize the ingredients you already possess, and those that you have yet to acquire. As you acquire that knowledge, you will also gain experience. Many times, you learn more through the search for knowledge than what you set out to learn in the first place.

It's important to be brutally honest about where you currently reside in the financial universe. By Taking Inventory, you're in the best position you could be in to improve your life. However, you don't have to be in a financial crisis to benefit from taking a closer look at your life. Those who take time for introspection are usually glad they did.

◆ ◆ ◆

It's time for you to understand what has held you back. Without this understanding, it's as if you're about to set out on an epic hike around the world, only to find that you have holes in your shoes before you even start – like your upbringing, your beliefs, or your communication skills.

You don't know what you don't know. The concept is more complex than you might think. Basically you know there's something flawed with your thinking, your habits, and/or your environment, but you don't know how to fix it. We grow up within the confines of our minds and our experiences, which creates biases in our thinking. It's hard to make an attachment to a new idea if you have no frame of reference for it. It's almost as if you've put on a piece of clothing that doesn't fit. Maybe it's too big, maybe it's too small, but either way, you can't wear it.

You know you should be able to change your life, but you don't know what's been holding you back. How can you fix something you can't see? Most often you just need someone to hold up a mirror so you can see your situation as it is. Without doing this one exercise, you have no idea what your life looks like.

James 1:23-24

> *Anyone who listens to the word but does not do what it says is like someone who looks at his face in a mirror and, after looking at himself, goes away and immediately forgets what he looks like.* (NIV)

In the case of this book, I'm the person holding up the mirror for you. You might not like what you see at first. It might even be shocking, but at least now you have an opportunity to do something about it.

The first thing to look at is how you manage money. This is important in life, but it's even more crucial in business. If you can't control your spending, there is no need to worry about being successful.

My clients pay me $50,000 to advise them one-on-one and I am told that the first phone call is brutal. During this call, I ask some hard-hitting and uncomfortable questions to help them take inventory of their present situation. It's surprising what I learn in that one phone call.

Some haven't filed taxes in years. Some have no investments at all. They have no actual accounting system or budget. Some have no idea how much they spend or how much debt they have. I often wonder, "In light of your current financials, how on earth did you come up with the $50,000 for the consultation? Did you rob a bank?"

One client told me, "After that first call, I was exhausted. It was so emotionally draining, I had to go take a nap." She's right. It's exhausting being in financial turmoil. Yet knowing what your true financial picture is, is the first step to turning it around.

◆ ◆ ◆

Every aspect of your life has been a choice. As I said in the introduction, I believe that God places us in circumstances, situations and environments to bless us, teach us, or reach us. Ultimately, though, we choose the outcome.

Here's an all-to-common and unfortunate illustration. Someone goes out to a nightclub and drinks too much. They then drive home, get pulled over, get a ticket, and subsequently a DUI on their record. This results in a negative background check which can result in all sorts of negative fallout. Yet, the bottom line is that this person chose to get drunk and drive and now they are stuck with the consequences.

In spite of this, many people want to blame other people for their mistakes. They don't see that what they do has a very direct and sometimes painful cause and effect. That doesn't mean I don't have compassion for those who have made poor choices. I do. I understand that we all make mistakes, sometimes devastating ones, but in the end, like I said, everything is a choice.

What's important in all this is to own up to what you've done and take responsibility for your actions. Once you face the fact that your life is a product of choices, if you aren't happy with where you are, you can stop and consciously choose to go another direction. You can begin to control your life.

If you acknowledge that ultimately you are in control of your life, it puts you in the driver's seat. While that may seem scary at first to take on all that responsibility, later on it will empower you to take on bigger challenges and reap greater rewards.

◆ ◆ ◆

This is a good place to mention the three Ds: dishonesty, deception, and denial. Most people suffer to some degree from all three.

I have never met anyone who is completely, one-hundred percent honest with themselves. Small deceptions grow into denial. When you deceive yourself, you are being dishonest. When you are dishonest with yourself, you are actually in denial.

The truth is, you can't really deceive yourself. You know the truth. You just choose to tell yourself a lie and then pretend that you believe it. It becomes a vicious cycle that leads to more deception, more dishonesty, and more denial. You get to a point that you're in denial that you're in denial. Living this way is a complete waste of energy. It's so much better to embrace the truth, even when it hurts.

I'll use a story I heard as an example. There once was a man who was getting counseling because he had a habit of hitting his wife when he was angry. He said, "My wife makes me so mad sometimes that I just can't help it. I haul off and slap her."

His counselor replied, "You're deceiving yourself. You're simply a bully and like most bullies, you're also a coward. You could control yourself if you really wanted to and I can prove it."

The man said, "But you don't know how things are between me and my wife. How can you prove that I can really control myself?"

The counselor looked the man up and down and quietly said, "The truth is, if you were in a room with Mike Tyson or some other heavy weight boxing champion and he made you mad, there is no way you would haul off and slap him no matter what he said or did. Even if he made you furious, you wouldn't slap him. You know that if you did, he'd beat the living daylights out of you and if you woke up at all, you'd wake up in the hospital. I guarantee you'd keep your temper in check, even if he kept on doing whatever it was that made you mad in the first place. In fact, you probably wouldn't even let on that you were angry at all.

"Or if there was some guy holding a gun to your head. I guarantee you wouldn't slap him either. You wouldn't even cuss him out. The only reason you slap your wife is because you're a bully. You know she won't hit you back and even if she did, you know it most likely wouldn't really hurt you."

When the counselor coached it in those terms, the man looked like someone punched him in the stomach. He said, "You're right. I am a bully and I've been a coward, hiding behind the lie that I can't control my temper. I see now that if I wanted to I could have controlled myself all along."

The counselor nodded his head and said, "The truth is, you're lucky your wife hasn't divorced you yet."

The man shrugged and said, "I wouldn't blame her if she did."

◆ ◆ ◆

Lots of people are in the habit of doing whatever their emotions tell them to do, which can be really scary if the person is an emotional basket case. This is especially important when making decisions, which should be based more on logic, than emotion. Emotions can crowd out objectivity if you let them, especially where anger is concerned (as evidenced in the story before). Always keep your thoughts in line and your emotions under control.

◆ ◆ ◆

Along the same lines, some people try to build themselves up by pulling others down. This is incredibly unproductive behavior. It produces nothing. The truth is, the only person who can bring you down is you. Likewise, the only person you can raise up is you. You can't even help someone else unless they truly want help. It they don't, again, you're wasting your time.

This reminds me of a story about a donkey that fell into a well. The townspeople kept throwing garbage into the well and as they did, the donkey trampled it under foot. Little by little the garbage got so high that the donkey was able to jump out of the well.

Life can be like that. If it seems that life is constantly throwing garbage on you, be like the donkey and use the resolve it takes to trample it down to raise yourself up.

◆ ◆ ◆

Unfortunately, there are obstacles to success. When some people encounter any kind of roadblock, they simply quit. The minute they come up against it, they're done. It's as if they were looking for an excuse as to why they couldn't, shouldn't, or wouldn't succeed. Without tenacity, any obstacle at all is the end of the road.

Tenacity is an invaluable commodity, but it can't be taught. It comes from within. Either you have it, or you don't. Yet, don't lose heart. If you don't have it now, you can acquire it. It simply requires that you keep going past all the places you usually stumble and stop.

♦ ♦ ♦

Success in business is often dependent on long-term relationships. At the end of the day, you don't have to know a lot of people to be successful, but you do need to know the right people. The problem is there are only so many hours in the day, and only so many time slots available to squeeze commitments into. To a large extent, who and what you put in those slots will dictate how successful you are. So, an important question to ask yourself – was the time I spent with that particular person a good investment or a waste of time?

It's been said that you are the sum total of the five people you spend the most time with. Here's an exercise that will prove enlightening: list those five people. Then, beside their names, put down what you think their annual income is. Add those numbers together, and then divide the sum by five. Guess what the usual outcome is? It will be the same as your annual income within a 10% margin.

So, then the question becomes, what if I remove one person and insert a person making $10 million a year? What does that do for your outlook? It changes the picture. What if you replace more people on your list with those that are more successful? It will significantly alter your financial picture.

Yet, most people aren't willing or courageous enough to make those kinds of changes. Their social circle becomes a boundary, and that essentially closes the path to growth and progress. Many people would rather be complacent and borderline broke, than face their insecurities to meet new people and make new friends, even if they knew that meant they would have all the potential up-side in the world.

Even if they are willing to try, most people aren't in a position to cultivate new friendships with those in a different income level. The average work-place is like a jar of pickles and all the employees are in the jar soaking in the brine along with all the other employees. They are stuck in the "go to work, sit in my cubicle, go home, five days a week" grind. It's not like there's a match website where you can log in to befriend a millionaire. Although it may be difficult to find them, that doesn't negate the need for exposure to those who are more successful than you are. You need to get out of the pickle jar and find an alternate way to grow.

For most people that situation is the norm. It's the choice they made and the way they live. If that's what you've chosen, then you shouldn't complain or whine. You shouldn't say, "My life sucks. My boss is a jerk. I don't get paid enough, etcetera." You're in this "pickle" because you chose it.

Instead try this: intern with a successful businessperson. Say to an entrepreneur, "You don't have to pay me. Just let me follow you around for three months. I'll be your assistant." And see what happens.

Not enough people are willing to do that. They're focused on their immediate needs. They are stuck trading hours for dollars and thinking, "What are you going to pay me now?"

In that kind of transaction, the employer says, "I'll give you X if you'll do Y." There is no ownership or partnership in this equation. You're just an employee. What people don't realize is that instead of investing in themselves, they're selling themselves for cheap. That may be harsh, when it comes to taking inventory, there's no room for anything less than brutal honesty.

There is a lot of peer pressure to stay with the tried and true. Heaven forbid you try something new that goes belly-up. If you do, your peer group may use you as target practice or a cautionary tale of why they stay in the status quo. If this is the case, my advice to you is to get a new peer group. Gravitate toward people that encourage entrepreneurialism and celebrate your courage and even your failure. Don't associate with people who are simply apathetic to your success or pat you on the back for being complacent.

♦ ♦ ♦

To be successful, a person needs to go from saying, "I wish." To saying, "I will." It seems like a small change, but it makes all the difference in the world. Let's say you see a car you've always wanted. Do you think, "I wish I owned that" Or do you say, "I will own that." Again, how you think and what you say makes all the difference in the world. You are thinking and speaking your life into existence. It says in the Bible, from the abundance of your heart, your mouth speaks.

Luke 6:45

> *A good man brings good things out of the good stored up in his heart, and an evil man brings evil things out of the evil stored up in his heart. For the mouth speaks what the heart is full of.* (NIV)

So, are you bringing about the good things or the bad?

♦ ♦ ♦

I think if you boiled down all the individual reasons people don't succeed, you would have one over-arching issue, fear of moving forward without seeing where the path leads or where it ends. What people don't realize is that the path doesn't end until you're dead. Life is constantly moving so it's much better if you choose to go where you want to go and to constantly move in a forward trajectory.

It's been said that even the longest journey begins with the first step. In the case of The Circle of Wealth, that's definitely true. However, it's fairly common that people look for reasons why they shouldn't take the first step, especially if it requires them to take a risk. It's that unwillingness to move forward without knowing what's ahead which blocks their path. It becomes a Catch-22. You won't move forward until you know what's going to happen, but you can't know what's going to happen until you move forward. So, instead, you don't budge and you're stuck.

The Bible says, don't worry about tomorrow for a reason.

Matthew 6:34

> *Therefore do not worry about tomorrow, for tomorrow will worry about itself. Each day has enough trouble of its own.* (NIV)

The only way to conquer fear is to face what you're afraid of head-on. People who know me have a hard time believing that I used to have a fear of public speaking. Some have said, "Lee, you're a natural speaker," but there is nothing further from the truth. I struggled with stage fright all my life and only overcame it with hard work and a lot of practice. I invested time and money into classes, books, and mentors who all taught me how to become an effective speaker. Even to this day, I continue to look for ways, mediums, and mentors to help me improve upon my public speaking. By studying the subject, I eliminated many of the "unknowns" and most of the fears and I was able to move forward with my goal. You can too.

◆ ◆ ◆

Common wisdom says that knowledge is power. The truth is, knowledge isn't power. It's potential power. Knowledge is only powerful when it's put to use.

Acquiring knowledge, then applying it to a problem is how you gain the kind of experience that will propel you forward toward success. It's been said that practice makes perfect. When you practice doing something, you gain experience and that experience leads to expertise, which people will pay you big bucks for it. You can enhance your likelihood of success by becoming really knowledgeable in a narrow field, rather than having a little bit of knowledge about a lot of things.

Along the same lines, some people think that they have to be super smart and have the degrees to prove it to be really successful. Truthfully, you don't. I'll be the first to admit that I'm not always the "smartest" guy in the room. In some circles, because I'm a college dropout, I would be considered one of the dumbest, but there is a vast difference between book smarts and intelligence. Let me paraphrase the Webster's Dictionary definition of the word "intelligence" to having the power to deal with a situation, especially a new situation successfully by making adjustments in behavior. True intelligence is having the ability to understand the interrelationships of facts, and to use them to problem solve and take action toward a desired goal.

It can be a real stumbling block for people who think that they need a degree in a certain field, a certificate in a specific industry, or a staggering resume of experience to succeed in life. In truth, none of those are a guarantee of success. In my opinion, intelligence isn't something you "have," rather it's something you "use" to make decisions about the various situations you're presented with. You then use your abilities to carry out those decisions. Intelligence isn't about having knowledge, but rather it's about how you use your knowledge, talents, and abilities wisely.

Words that convey this idea of intelligence are: observing, thinking, understanding, applying, acting, and doing. As you can see, it's a long way from memorizing something from a textbook.

Don't get me wrong, books are important, but they are only important as the actions they inspire. You can read all the motivational books in the world, but they will do you absolutely no good unless you do something with what you have read. It's not what the writer puts into a book that's most important, it's what you take out of it that matters.

So, intelligence is just a starting point. You should also factor in your life experience. What have you done? What was successful? What wasn't? What did you learn?

That said, while intelligence isn't the most important factor, it's still a factor. In the analysis of any opportunity, it's crucial to be brutally honest with yourself about how much you know and how much you can reasonably learn before going into a venture. If you're working with less knowledge about the field you're interested in, you're going to have to compensate by bringing in business partners, employees, or even friends and family (but only if they can be brutally honest with you).

In the same neighborhood as intelligence is education. To be successful in business, education is a nicety, although not necessarily a requirement. Often people are over-reliant on education, or on the flip-side, they use the lack of an education as a reason not to pursue an opportunity. A college degree doesn't define a person, nor does it dictate the likelihood of success or failure in business. You can have a stellar education and be smart as a whip, but still make idiotic business decisions and never make a decent living.

Here's how I personally approach Taking Inventory of my educational strengths and weaknesses before going into a business venture. Let's say I want to build a house with the intention to sell it. First I'm going to need land to build on. I have my real estate license, so I can take care of buying the land myself. Next, I'll need some plans. I'm not an architect and I don't want to take the time to learn to be one, so I'll hire someone to draw up the plans for me. Next, comes the foundation. I've poured cement before, but not a whole foundation, so I'll need to hire someone to do that too. Next comes framing. I've done some framing in my day and I actually enjoy doing it, but with my travel and work schedule, if I plan on getting the house done before the next ice-age, I'm going to have to hire someone to help me. You get the idea.

Take any opportunity apart and look at every facet of it realistically, just like I did with building the house. Can you do it with your present skill-set? Do you have time to do it? Do you have time or want to learn what you don't know? Or, can you hire or partner with someone who already has the necessary skill-set and can shave off the time and headaches it would take for you to learn how to do it yourself?

When you've answered those questions, we can reasonably say that you have some wisdom about the opportunity. Wisdom is the by-product of employing intelligence, knowledge, and education effectively.

♦ ♦ ♦

In the game of business, it's crucial to figure out whether you're a racehorse or a jockey. In this analogy, a business opportunity or an entrepreneur is usually called the horse, while company executives and managers are referred to as jockeys.

If you're betting on the education and skill of a management team, you're betting on the jockey. If you're betting on an idea and an entrepreneur's unbridled passion and willingness to beat the competition out of the gate, regardless of education, then your money is on the horse. Either way it's a gamble.

Obviously, the best-case scenario is that you have both – a great jockey riding a fantastic horse or an entrepreneur who is both a horse and a jockey.

If you're like me and you don't have a higher education, then you're a racehorse. In some ways, being the horse is the harder route because you have to prove that you can win and win almost every time. It will be hard to get anyone to bet on you until you've proven that you can win consistently. That being the case, you'd better plan on being a workhorse to make things happen.

The advantage that you have being a winning horse is that you can hire a jockey. In fact, you can hire a whole locker room full of them. I'm a racehorse who has employed a lot of jockeys—MBAs, CPAs, CFOs, attorneys, you name it. If you're a jockey, all you need is a diploma, preferably from an impressive school, to get the best position you can find. Then you simply do a good job for your employer and move up the ladder. A college education is simply an indicator that a person can satisfactorily complete a task within a given time frame. They've spent eighteen years proving that if you tell them what to do, and when to do it, they will do it. However, in general, they don't make great entrepreneurs. They've spent so long in that educational box, they need someone to tell them what to do and when to do it.

That's not to say I have anything against jockeys. I don't. I couldn't run my business without them. It's just that my heart is with the racehorses.

◆ ◆ ◆

Occasionally a client will tell me they want to achieve a more prosperous future, but they don't have any idea as to how to go about it. This is a roadblock that is more real than many of the things people consider barriers to their success.

At the center of all entrepreneurial endeavors is "the idea." Read any biography or autobiography about a successful entrepreneur and somewhere in the first few chapters, they will say something like, "I had an idea..." Or, "Something came to me..." Or, "I developed a concept..."

An idea is like the seed of your future and everything you do to bring that idea to fruition is like the germination of the seed.

All that said, if you want to be entrepreneurial but you honestly don't have a fresh idea for a business, then think about investing in a franchise. With a franchise someone had an idea, which worked well enough that it can be reliably reproduced. It has a proven business model, business plan, and operational procedures already in place, so you don't have to reinvent the wheel. The only caveat when investing in a franchise is to make sure it's a good fit for your strengths and interests. It's imperative to identify what those are before you invest.

It all goes back to "Taking Inventory." What do you like to do? Do you like working with people? Are you good with numbers? Do you want to provide a service?

A great thing about going into a franchise is that you can get bank financing to buy one. It's much easier to get the start-up capital for a franchise than for an unproved business model. The cost averages between $25,000 to $100,000, depending on the franchise, which isn't much when you consider that you're not just buying a business, you're buying a future.

♦ ♦ ♦

Another issue that trips people up is not having start-up capital, or money to invest. To that I say, "Good." Lack of start-up capital is not a liability. It can actually be an asset, but only if you'll allow it to be.

You may think I'm crazy, but let me explain. Eighty-six percent of all new businesses fail within the first two years. Why? In my opinion, it's because they have easy access to too much readily available cash.

People who have all the capital they need to get going in a business venture, often don't do their due diligence to investigate all facets of it beforehand. If they don't take it apart and examine what's involved, they likely won't understand what will be required of them to succeed at the venture. They might not realize how much time it will take before they turn a profit. They may not know whether they have the skill-set they'll need to expand. They might not know who to hire or how to delegate certain tasks. They may not have enough money for ongoing expenses or infusions of capital. The list could go on and on.

Say you have $1 million in the bank and you want to buy the grand-daddy of all franchises, a McDonald's®. The franchise costs $250,000, but because you have $1 million in the bank, you can buy the franchise outright. However, $250,000 is just the tip of the iceberg. There are build-out costs, legal fees, payroll, etcetera. By the time you pay for it all, you'll be running out of money. In fact, shortly after you open the doors you'll be tapped out.

Now, if you didn't have enough money in the bank to buy that McDonald's ® franchise outright, then you had to put together a business plan, a marketing plan, and a group of investors. You had to make a bank believe in you enough to give you a loan. You had to knock on a thousand doors and have most of them slammed in your face. You had to be rejected over and over again. Yet, during all of this, you were honing your skills, learning your strengths, and discovering your weaknesses. You were polishing your business plan, putting together a solid team, and creating a network of strategic relationships.

That's why I say a lack of start-up capital can be an asset. It will force you to acquire the skill-set that you'll need to be successful in business. You'll gain communication skills, selling expertise, and negotiation chops. It's really the best business education out there.

These are just some of the points to think about, and some of the questions to ask in "Taking Inventory." You may have to invest some time in it. The answers may not come easily and the truth might not be easy to face. But, take it from me, the time you spend learning to understand yourself will benefit you more, and bring greater returns, than almost anything else.

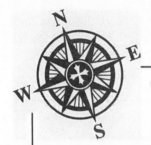

51.4 Degrees of
Taking Inventory

1. Learn to be honest with yourself about who you are.
2. Learn to find your own solutions to problems.
3. Take stock of your strengths and weaknesses.
4. Learn to compensate for weaknesses and enhance your strengths.
5. Pick goals that fit you.

WRITE DOWN 10 STRENGTHS AND 10 WEAKNESSES.

STRENGTHS & ASSETS	WEAKNESSES & LIABILITIES
Good Communicator	*Poor Money Manager*

PART 2
MY VENTURE

The summer I turned seventeen I started working for the Parks Department, as well as Yoke's market and Avis Rent-a-Car.

I worked at the Park's Department from 8:00 AM to 4:00 PM Monday through Friday. Then I went to Yoke's and worked from 5:00 PM until 2:00 AM and on weekends I worked at Avis from 8:00 AM to 5 PM.

At the Parks Department, I worked at Spokane's Cannon Hill Park and basically played games like Capture the Flag or Kick the Can with the kids all day. I also coached two t-ball teams and a baseball team and had to drive the kids to their games. At the time, I didn't have my own car, so I was driving my father's pick-up truck.

One day as I was leaving my Parks Department job to go to Yoke's, I put the key in the ignition and it snapped off. I had to find a phone booth and call my father for help.

I'll never forget his response. He said, "Lee, how old are you?"

"Seventeen," I said.

He then said, "That's right. You're old enough to figure it out for yourself" and then he hung up.

I couldn't believe it. I had to rummage in my pockets for another quarter to call a locksmith, wait for an hour for him to come and fix the truck, and then get myself to work late. The next morning my father walked into my room and said, "I see you got the truck fixed."

"No thanks to you," I said with a scowl. He smiled and said, "You'll thank me later."

Guess what? My father was right. I figured it out. And I continue to thank him for forcing me out of my comfort zone to learn how to problem solve. If he would have taken care of the problem for me, I wouldn't have learned anything. Learning to figure things out for myself was just as important to my success as learning how to work hard.

Another thing I learned that year was the value of giving. The management at Yoke's tried to persuade all their workers to volunteer at Thanksgiving that year by serving dinner at a local soup kitchen.

Although I was only a bag boy at the time, I said, "I'll go."

When I showed up to volunteer, guess who were the only people there? The management – the president of the company, the CEO, the CFO, the COO, and all the store managers. I didn't know it at the time, but the management was really impressed that a young kid who only made $3.90 an hour took time from his family on Thanksgiving to help at the soup kitchen.

As a result of investing my time, when there was an opening for a checker, I was offered the position and when a merchandising display manager position opened, I was promoted again and then again when a new store opened up. I believe this all happened because I took the time to serve mashed potatoes and gravy to homeless people on Thanksgiving. Generosity and authenticity make a huge difference in the world of business.

So, not only did I learn to think for myself that year, I also learned that some of the greatest rewards in business, and in life, come through giving.

PART 1
SETTING THE GOAL

If you're ready to move ahead, the next step is to ask yourself what you want to achieve in your life. It should be a clear and tangible objective. The answer to that question is your goal. If you've done your homework from the previous section, you won't be setting a goal that's unrealistic or doesn't fit you.

To give yourself the greatest chance of success, make sure your goal has three points.

One – you truly desire it.

Two – you believe you can achieve it.

Three – it is achievable.

It's not that your goal shouldn't be a stretch. In fact, it's good if it is. But it shouldn't be out of the realm of possibility, like me becoming a prima ballerina, for example. No matter how hard I worked at it, it "ain't gonna happen". Although that's a glaringly obvious example, you get the idea.

That's why taking an honest inventory of your likes and dislikes, your gifts and talents, and strengths and weaknesses is so important. If you've done that, you can choose your goals accordingly and save yourself a whole lot of grief going after a goal that really doesn't suit you. For example, it would make no sense for someone who dislikes dealing with people to go into a service-based business where dealing with people is a requirement. They would do much better in something like accounting, where they sit behind a desk crunching numbers and pushing papers.

Speaking of accounting, here's another example. Let's say a friend who is a real estate developer calls me up and says, "Hey, Lee, I've got a great idea. Let's start an accounting firm."

My first response is, "What?"

He replies, "Well, I received a bill from my accountant and there's lots of money in accounting."

I think about the last bill I received from my accountant and say, "Yeah, you're right. There is a lot of money in accounting. We could probably make a pretty good living."

Without any further thought, my friend and I set out to start an accounting firm. Mind you that neither one of us enjoys accounting, is great with money, nor has a degree in financing. We don't even know how to work an Excel spreadsheet. However, we're really good at sales, so we start lining up clients for our new firm.

On my first sales call, the owner of the company says, "What we need is a structure utilizing Excel in multiple tabs so we can see the acceleration of base rates times nineteen months, including the appreciation of the assets, blah, blah, blah…" I have no idea what he's talking about.

I say, "Sure we can do that. I'll get a quote to you right away."

This scenario looks ridiculous on paper and you can see the Grand Canyon-sized hole in my logic. Yet, going into a business without any knowledge of, or preparation for, what that business actually entails happens more often than you might think. I believe it's the main reason more than eight out of ten businesses fail within the first eighteen months.

If I had taken inventory before starting my imaginary accounting firm, I would have realized that neither I, nor my friend, had any qualifications to successfully run that kind of company on our own.

That doesn't necessarily mean we can't start the business. Let's say, even though I hate doing accounting, it's always been my dream to own an accounting firm. If I've taken the time to do an in-depth evaluation, I may find that there is enough potential profit to hire capable accountants to run the business for me. I can hire people to compensate for the skills I'm lacking and because it's always been my dream, I'm willing to take the risk. Would it be better if my friend and I were accountants? Sure. But our lack of skill in that area doesn't rule us out as the owners of the business. All we really need to know is how to hire and manage honest, competent accountants, and have enough up-front capital to pay their salaries until the firm is able to.

That start-up money has to come from somewhere.

In this example, if my friend and I have been successful at our other businesses, then even without any accounting skills of our own, we would have a decided advantage over a fresh-out-of-college accountant who is trying to go into business for him or herself. We would already have the knowledge and experience, times two, of how to run a business. That experience and reputational capital is what will allow us to borrow the start-up capital from The Circle of Wealth and that's an advantage that you can't really buy, rather you earn it.

◆ ◆ ◆

In talking about setting a goal, let's also talk about opportunity. I think a problem many people face when entering The Circle is that they haven't taken time to really open their minds to all the opportunities that are available. If you aren't looking for opportunity, you can become blind to it. You won't even recognize it when it's right in front of your face. It's like the well-worn cliché says: you can't see the forest through the trees.

The power to recognize opportunity is found in saying, "That's what I want to do." Or, "That's who I want to be." It starts everything.

A lot of people think of opportunity as being a product of happenstance. To some degree it is, but not in a way that's really significant. If you've done your homework by "Taking Inventory," you'll have a greater chance of being in the right place at the right time, which is often just a matter of seeing things in a different light. An interesting thing happens when you set a goal and choose to believe you can achieve it. Suddenly you can see opportunity that was invisible before. If you know what you're looking for, you'll see possibilities where you once saw nothing but impossibilities.

Opportunities come in their own time. You should always be prepared to act if something comes your way. Some opportunities are once in a lifetime and to wait to act will postpone success, and sometimes lead to failing completely.

Opportunity can come in many forms and it's not always obvious, nor always financial. It could be someone willing to mentor you, coach you, or give you feedback on a business plan or your resume. It could be someone who wants to partner with you and is willing to give you seed money to start a business. Opportunity comes in all shapes and sizes and if you're open to it and able to discern it in the most unlikely places, you'll find that success is much easier to come by.

◆ ◆ ◆

Speaking of opportunity, I think it's amusing when one of my employees comes into my office and says, "Hey, Lee, I want to start investing in real estate. Can you give me some tips?"

This has happened more than once. It wouldn't be so amusing if it only happened with new employees, but most of the people who inquire have been with me for years. I always say, "Sure. Start by reading my curriculum in the big orange box called, *Fortunes in Foreclosure*. It's over there on the shelf that you've walked past, without noticing, ever since you started working here."

They generally look stunned. They haven't really thought about that course pertaining to them. It has only been something we have recommended to our clients over the phone or at seminars. Yet it, and all the other resources on the shelf, has been fully available to them the whole time they've worked for me. They have had free access to a wealth of knowledge, but because they see it every day, they don't realize the opportunity they have to tap into it and learn and profit from it. It's only when a person starts to think, "You know, I want to be successful too," do they begin to recognize what an opportunity looks like and in this case the opportunity came in the form of a big orange box sitting on our company book shelf.

So, if opportunity knocks, make sure you answer the door!

◆ ◆ ◆

It's important to understand that there is a great big financial universe out there and you can have as big a piece of it as you're willing to go after. It won't bankrupt the universe if you become wealthy. There is room for everyone. So don't be afraid to dream big.

In his book *Ultimate Success*, Dan Kennedy says something along the lines of, "You can go to the ocean with a spoon, a gallon bucket, or a super-tanker. And you can take out as much as your vessel can hold and no one will even notice." This analogy speaks of the abundance of wealth that's available to you.

When an entrepreneur creates a business, the world's financial pie isn't divided into smaller pieces. Instead, the size of the whole pie grows. If you think about it, when Warren Buffet made his $40 billion, were you negatively affected? When Bill Gates made $30 billion on Microsoft or when the other technology giants made their billions, did it affect you? The only effect was the creation of a whole new industry, which in turn creates jobs, ingenuity, and products for the greater good of society. In business, it's not a zero/sum game or an "either/or" scenario. In fact, like The Circle of Wealth, it's often a "blessing," where all involved can benefit.

◆ ◆ ◆

To reach your destination, like the billionaires we just talked about, you'll need to stay motivated.

It's been said that it takes more energy to overcome the inertia of a body at a standstill than it does to keep a body moving that is already in motion. It's a law of physics and it's true in the area of personal and professional motivation.

Motivation is a burning desire that will spur you into action to accomplish a goal. You may say, "Lee, I want to achieve my goal, but I'm just not ambitious."

I would argue that you are, you just haven't found the right motivator yet. It could be taking care of your family, getting ahead in your career, or pursuing an ideal. Psychologists say that people are motivated to action by one of two triggers – pain or pleasure. Make it your aim to understand what your main motivation is: pain or pleasure. Is it salary? Is it time off? Do you aim for recognition? Do you prefer a routine? Do you need a sense of security? The idea is to understand what motivates you and then create new habits based on that motivation.

If a person isn't motivated by the pleasure of accomplishing a goal, going on vacations, increasing his or her assets, or upgrading his or her lifestyle, then he or she may be motivated by pain. That pain often comes in the form of fear, like an anxiety of not getting ahead or not having enough money. Fear can be as strong a motivator as pleasure, though nowhere near as pleasant.

The pleasure trigger is pretty self-explanatory, but I think the pain trigger can bear an illustration. Here's how the pain motivation plays out in my business.

I charge $150,000 for three days of mentoring, counsel, and instruction with me. Some people have said, "How do you get off charging $150,000 for a three-day consultation?" Because, unfortunately, based on people's performance, their money is safer with me than it is with them. If I charge $150,000 that might be expensive enough that someone will actually pay attention and do what I say.

When I first started my mentoring program, I charged $15,000. At this rate, we would actually have people who paid for it in full, but never scheduled their consultation. We would practically beg them to arrange a time for the consultation and each time we would be met with a slew of excuses. Clearly, $15,000 wasn't painful enough. So, we raised the price to $25,000. Again, we had people who didn't schedule their consultation. So, I upped the cost to $50,000. Do you know, that right now there are two people who have paid for a $50,000 consultation and still haven't made time for it yet?

Now that the service is much more painful. At $150,000, we get much better results. There hasn't been a single person who hasn't scheduled their consultation.

◆ ◆ ◆

People have told me that I'm lucky because I have a great family, a nice house, and I live in a good neighborhood. I'm not lucky. I'm motivated. I'm motivated by where and how I want my family to live, which is in a good and safe neighborhood. I'm motivated by what I want to accomplish in my life.

When people say that they want the same thing, I always tell them that if they want to learn from my own experience, they first need to go to church on Sunday. That's a great place to begin. Then, they need to drive to the neighborhoods where they want to live in. They need to start looking at properties and start envisioning their lives there. They need to start thinking bigger.

For example, when my wife, Jaclyn, and I were looking for a house in Washington, we decided what neighborhood we wanted to live in and where we wanted to raise our children. We made it our goal and then channeled all of our efforts toward eventually moving there. For me, family is a very strong motivator. Likely for you, it's the same.

Let's say the neighborhood you're living in has a high crime rate. Your neighbors drink too much and smoke pot in their front yard. On top of this, their yards are littered with junk cars and garbage. It's not a great place to raise kids and you're motivated to get your children out of that environment.

Unfortunately, you're only making $12 an hour and your spouse makes about the same, but only works part-time to be home with the kids after school. You're struggling to get by and it's really tempting to believe that this is just the way life is and that's how it's always going to be.

However, that's not how it has to be. You have the power to change the way things are, and your children's future needs to be your prime motivation. The desire to move out of a bad situation will subconsciously start you thinking more creatively and suddenly the opportunities will begin to pop up. You'll see jobs in the newspaper you hadn't noticed or homes for sale or rent in areas you never thought were possible. You'll discover new ways to hit your target. Things will begin to change.

♦ ♦ ♦

When you step out to try something new, many times an uneasy feeling will come over you, and you will hesitate. That's a natural response to protect you from potential danger. It's an instinct that has been developed over thousands of years and we all have it to a degree. The problem comes when the instinct for protection becomes crippling.

Even though a person may have a fear of the unknown, if they have a strong enough desire to achieve their goal, they will override that fear. Yes, it's a gamble, but only if you try. If you don't try, you're not gambling at all because failure to reach your goal is guaranteed.

♦ ♦ ♦

Start where you are.

Zechariah 4:10

> *Do not despise these small beginnings, for the Lord rejoices to see the work begin. . .* (NLT)

I'm the founder of a multi-million dollar company, but it didn't begin that way. I started my company in my house. We turned a bedroom in the basement into an office and my first assistant sat next to me at a makeshift desk. We went upstairs to the living room for our executive meetings, quarterly meetings, and annual meetings, which consisted of my assistant, me, and my wife.

You'd be hard-pressed to find an entrepreneur, CEO, founder, famous public speaker, or anyone else who is successful, who didn't have to start somewhere and work to achieve that success. It's the same with any dream or goal. You can't get anywhere near where you want to go, unless you begin. It's really simple, but you would not believe how many people are defeated long before they even begin.

♦ ♦ ♦

Just because you've taken an honest look at your life and you're setting a goal, doesn't mean you've made any headway. In fact, unless something miraculous happened, nothing has changed and the reality of how far you have to go is looming in front of you like a mountain range. That said, I want to add this: under no circumstances should you let that discourage you.

An important step in your journey is to make the decision that once you've set your mind on a goal, you will not allow yourself the luxury of being discouraged – no matter what.

Don't be afraid to take on big challenges. Look at them as opportunities. Yes, it's scary to face a big challenge, but just remember that the things you fear about facing the tests and trials are probably the same things other people fear as well. That's what makes a challenge an opportunity. If you don't allow those fears to stop you, you'll find yourself going places most people don't go and you'll get there easier than you imagined, simply because there isn't as much competition.

The bottom line is, when confronted with a challenge, you should always ask, "How can I _____" and then fill in the blank.

It's a good idea to break challenges down into smaller segments. Identify something you can accomplish fairly easily. It's important to build confidence in your ability by achieving smaller tasks. By breaking it down into segments, you will have a chance to get used to the feeling of success. It's almost impossible to know all that will be required to reach your goal, but I know from experience, you can always take the next step.

Only you can choose your goals. Only you know what you need to do to feel fulfilled in life. Only you know what opportunities are available to you and only you can say yes, or no, to the opportunities that are presented.

So, start now. Whatever you want to do, start now. There's absolutely no reason to wait.

51.4 Degrees of
Setting the Goal

1. Start where you are.
2. Know what you want to accomplish in your life.
3. Find the motivation to accomplish it.
4. Conquer your fear by eliminating unknowns.
5. Don't get discouraged by challenges.

I WANT TO BE HEALTHY, WEALTHY, AND SUCCESSFUL BECAUSE ...
(must be 800 characters.)

_____

_____

_____

_____

_____

_____

_____

_____

_____

_____

_____

_____

_____

_____

_____

_____

PART 2
MY VENTURE

When I turned eighteen, I graduated from high school, quit my summer jobs at Avis and the Parks Department and began going to college. I went to Spokane Falls Community College from 8:00 AM until noon and then worked at Yoke's Market from 3 PM to midnight. I would often get home around 1:30 AM.

Keeping those hours, I didn't have much of a social life, and by the time I got home, all that was on TV were infomercials. One infomercial in particular that piqued my interest was about buying and selling real estate. They said it was the quickest way to gain wealth. It was also driving the at-home audience (me) to a free seminar in Spokane. Because the seminar was in the middle of the day, I had to take a day off of work to attend, but I decided it was worth it because I wanted to learn how to buy and sell real estate. I wanted the quickest way to gain wealth too.

I was starting to form a goal.

I went to the seminar, which low and behold, between all the talks and slick PowerPoints, was nothing more than a sales pitch for a $1,598 course that would teach me how to make a fortune in real estate. All I had to do was go to the back table and write them a check.

The problem was, I didn't have $1,598. But using my father's logic that I was old enough to figure out how to get the money, I went to the back table and wrote them a check. I said, "If you cash this tomorrow, it'll bounce, but if you hold it for seven days, I'll figure out how to get the money.

Amazingly, they agreed.

So the next day, I went around to all the departments at the grocery store – the bakery, the meat department, the produce section – hoping someone would loan me the money for the seminar. I was rejected nine times. When I finally went to the pharmacist, Brent, he said, "I won't lend you the money, but if you go to the seminar and learn everything you need to know and you find a good property, we'll use my credit to buy and fix it up."

Brent was willing to help me get started on my journey, but I still needed $1,598 for the course. That night we had a family birthday party and I asked everyone there for a loan. No one in my family would give me the money either.

In an act of desperation, I did what I'd never advise anyone to do and I called my bank, Cheney Credit Union, for a loan.

After asking if I had any credit or a credit card, the loan agent asked me if I had any assets. At the time I had a pick-up that the Credit Union and loaned me money for. When she looked at my loan, she found that I had built up $3,000 in equity in my pick-up.

I took the money, deposited it, and the $1,598 check cleared a few days later. I went to the three-day seminar, but I was quick to learn that the $1,598 was just the tip of the iceberg. At the seminar, they had all types of items for sale ranging from software priced at $2,800 to personal coaching for $25,000. They claimed that if I wanted to be successful in real estate, I would need all of it. Unfortunately I couldn't afford any of it. I told myself, "Even though I don't have the money, somehow I'll figure this out."

Instead I bought every book I could get my hands on about real estate and I started studying. I wrote notes in the front, the back, and in the margins of each book. I noted the main points, ideas that came to me, questions I had, and I wrote a journal of what was happening in my life at the time. To keep from getting discouraged, in more than one book I wrote, "I will figure this out."

I can't tell you how many times I prayed, "God, give me the opportunities and capital to realize this dream." At the time I remember my pastor gave a sermon that said, "God answers prayers in three ways. Yes. No. And grow."

When I asked God for money and it didn't show up, I didn't believe he was saying, "No, Lee, you can't do this." Every time the mailbox, my bank account, or my pockets were empty, I chose to believe that it was His way of saying, "Grow." I interpreted it as Him saying, "Lee, you're not ready to handle that much money. You need to learn to manage your finances. You need wisdom. You need common sense. You need understanding." And He was right.

PART 1
BUILDING A STRATEGY

Now you've set your goal. So naturally, you want to start moving toward it. You're excited and you're motivated. However, it's imperative that you have a workable plan or strategy in place before you go full bore. No one plans to fail, they just fail to plan. So let's get a strategy in place.

Before you start forming a strategy to reach your goal, make sure you've finished "Taking Inventory." Yes, I'm going back to that again. I've been at this awhile and I know how human nature works. "Taking Inventory" isn't fun and many people try to skip the painful work that needs to be done first. I know this because, in the past, I would have done the same thing. However, there is a swamp hidden in the center of The Circle of Wealth. If you haven't taken inventory, more likely than not, you won't understand your weaknesses and you'll fall into the swamp. But if you follow the path that I'm laying out for you, it will help you reach your destination.

◆ ◆ ◆

Every business will need to have its own tailor-made strategy and you will have to do your homework to put one in place. I can't build a winning strategy for you from the pages of this book. More in-depth input would be required and we would need to have a serious talk about a one-on-one consultation. What I can do, though, is point out some of the things that you should think about as you're putting together the building blocks to your goal.

To a large degree, you will have to figure your business strategy out for yourself. Even if you have the help of advisors, most of the strategy will come from you. By definition, the word entrepreneur carries the connotation of self-reliance. So you may as well start now.

Begin forming your strategy with the end in mind. Or put another way, begin with your ultimate goal in mind. As you make choices, fast-forward to the end-goal and envision how well those decisions fit into the picture. Will it take you closer to the goal or move you farther away?

It's also important to have incremental plans. You should have a one year, five year, and ten year plan for your business. Like "Taking Inventory" in Chapter 2, many people try to skip Chapter 4 and rush right into the execution of their goal. Believe me, I know from personal experience that it never works. How on earth can you implement a non-existent strategy?

♦ ♦ ♦

The lines between a goal and the strategy are sometimes blurred. For the most part, even if you have a specific goal in mind, it's still somewhat general. The strategy deals with the details. Most likely your strategy will change as you progress toward your goal, but it's important that you have one to begin with. If you take the time to plan, your work in the future will be partly done.

Here's a simple illustration of a goal versus a strategy: let's say you want to buy a house. That's your goal. First you would contact a realtor, who will ask a lot of strategic questions, like "How much do you want to spend? What neighborhood do you want to live in? What size house do you want? How many bedrooms? How many baths? What size property? Do you want acreage?" The answers to those questions will help your realtor choose which houses to show you. All of that is a strategy.

On the flip-side, imagine a family road trip where you load the car with suitcases, the dog, and the kids. When you're ready to go, one of the kids asks, "Where are we going?" You reply, "I don't know, but I'm sure glad we got everything in the car."

That's what it's like moving forward on a strategy without a specific goal in mind. Believe it or not, people do that sort of thing in business all the time. It's more common than you might think.

Someone says, "I want to start a business."

Then someone else asks, "What kind of business. What do you want to do?"

The person replies, "I'm not sure yet."

Well, you'd better not pack the suitcases then!

Begin with the end in mind. Where do you want to go with this business? Answer that, and then start drawing a roadmap to get there.

When you say, "I'm going to _____", and you take time to plan your strategy, then parts of that plan will begin to come together and reaching your goal will become more conceivable, more plausible, and much easier to accomplish. A detailed strategy opens your eyes to all the facets of your objective everywhere.

Here's an example: a few years ago I decided that I wanted a Toyota Tacoma pick-up truck. Before I made the decision, I never noticed Tacomas on the road or in parking lots. However, once I decided I wanted one, suddenly there were Toyota Tacomas everywhere. In fact, my next-door neighbor had a one that I had never even noticed it until I made my decision.

I believe success is the same way. Once you recognize what it is that you want, the tools, the contacts, the relationships, and the opportunities start presenting themselves to you. Actually, they were there the whole time, but it wasn't until you said, "That's what I want to do," or, "That's who I want to be," or "That's what I want to have," that they suddenly became apparent.

The strategy is knowing what you want to do, how you want to do it, and when you want to do it.

◆ ◆ ◆

Let's say one of your goals was similar to one of mine—to be a real estate investor. As an investor, you need to decide what kind of investor you want to be—commercial or residential. Are you planning to invest locally or nationwide? Do you want to wholesale, fix and flip, or hold and rent out your properties? All the above are strategic questions.

In order to help you understand this better, and how I help my clients figure out their specific goals in real estate, I'll create a fictional prospective real estate investor, who we'll call "Cathy." The first thing I ask Cathy is, "Do you want to be a commercial or residential investor?"

Cathy pauses a moment and then says, "I think I want to be a commercial investor and buy large apartment buildings."

Right away, I'm sure she doesn't have a strategy. If she did, she wouldn't use the word "think," she would know.

My next question is, "Have you ever bought a piece of real estate before?"

Cathy replies, "No. Not yet."

Bingo. I was right. She has no real estate experience.

My response is, "You've never bought property and you want to start with a multi-million dollar deal? That's not a very sound idea."

Cathy looks dejected. Now, I'm not trying to hurt her feelings and I'm not trying to kill her dreams. I'm doing her a favor. It's not that she can't be a commercial real estate investor, it's just that she can't be one without having a strategy to become one.

So, I say, "Cathy, don't be discouraged. You can eventually buy apartment buildings, but you need to start smaller and build up enough working capital so that goal is more feasible. Buy five single-family homes this year and either wholesale or fix and flip them. With this strategy, depending on the deal, you should be able to net $100,000. Once you've done that, you'll be in a better position to start investing in commercial real estate."

I've left her with a real and actionable strategy that she can implement to start the journey toward her goal.

Now let's look at another industry. Maybe your goal is to open a restaurant. The questions are similar and the same principles apply. What kind of restaurant do you want to open—casual or fine dining? Where do you want to open it—in an established commercial district or an up-

and-coming neighborhood? Will that location fit the style of your restaurant? What kind of food—American, Asian, Mediterranean? Do you want it to be large or intimate and cozy? Will it be a franchise? Will you be the sole owner or will you have partners?

Then come the questions about financing. How will you fund your restaurant—a home equity line of credit, peer-to-peer funding, or credit cards? You get the idea. But don't go any further until you have answers to those questions.

◆ ◆ ◆

Money is attracted to opportunity and investors write checks based on a great story. People want to be part of something interesting, exciting, and growing. They want to be part of the next big thing. So, tell a good, and more importantly, true story about your ideas and what you want to accomplish and watch investors line up to invest. Honesty is everything in The Circle of Wealth and in most cases, you will only have one chance to do business with someone. If you burn them, you probably won't get another chance. Also, business doesn't occur in a bubble. Experienced investors usually know one another. If you burn one, who knows how many others they will tell and if you're a bad risk, pretty soon everyone will hear about it.

It's true that you can't guarantee success. You will make mistakes along the way, but to maintain your credibility, tell the truth first and then work your tail off to accomplish the milestones and goals you said you would in the first place. If you do that, the mistakes will often work themselves out.

◆ ◆ ◆

Another well-documented principle of success is if you want to be successful, you must appear successful. In other words, dress for success. That old adage is true. As you plan for success, plan to dress for success too. That goes not only for your clothes, but your hair, your speech, and your attitude. You want to be the complete package.

When it comes down to the wire, how you appear may make the difference between success and failure. For example, if an investor is sitting on the fence about investing, how you appear may sway the investor one way or the other. Make sure your appearance doesn't sway them in a direction you don't want them to go.

♦ ♦ ♦

One of my mentors once said, "Above your ears you generate wealth, below your ears you generate wages." Meaning, working with your hands, you earn wages, and get paid by the hour. Working with your mind, you can generate wealth and earn an unlimited income.

The biggest problem with working for wages is that there are only so many hours in a day. You can't make more hours, so you can only make more money in an hour.

For example, when I worked as a grocery store bag boy, I made $3.90 an hour. When I looked at my schedule, I could tell by how many hours they gave me, what my paycheck would be.

One way to bring in more money would be to go back to school, earn a degree, and land a management position. However, in doing so you also take on somewhere in the neighborhood of $20,000 in student loan debt just to earn an extra $5.00 an hour. You're also still in the rut of earning wages.

The idea is to get to a place where your money is working for you. That's the best way to insure continuity not only of income, but also of increase. The best way to do that is to leverage your time, talent, and income – or generating wealth above your ears.

The leverage you're looking for is to become an expert in your field. As I've said before, people will pay big money for expertise.

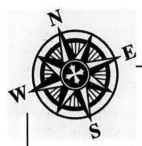

51.4 Degrees of
Building a Strategy

1. Know the difference between a goal and a strategy.
2. Break your goals into doable parts.
3. Make choices with the goal in mind.
4. Keep your word and don't burn investors.
5. Know when and how to hire help.

YOUR "STRENGTHS" COMBINED WITH YOUR "WHY" WILL EQUAL YOUR "MOTIVATION". IDENTIFY WHAT SKILL SETS YOU NEED TO HIRE FIRST. IT MAY BE SALES, ACCOUNTING, MARKETING, WRITING, OR WEB DESIGN. NEED + DON'T ENJOY = HIRE

Five things you need to start

_____

_____

_____

_____

_____

Five things you enjoy doing the most

_____

_____

_____

_____

_____

PART 2
MY VENTURE

PART 2
MY VENTURE

One specific and useful principle I learned from that first real estate seminar was how to write offers on "For Sale by Owner" properties. The rest, I had already learned from experience: that I would have to work hard, giving up wasn't an option, and I would have to figure things out for myself.

At the time, I had a three-hour break from 12 PM to 3 PM between getting home from college and going to work at the grocery store. At the store I had an hour break from 7 PM to 8 PM. I used those hours to call all the "For Sale by Owner" ads in the newspaper. I set the appointments to meet with the property owners on weekends.

I met with almost one hundred homeowners trying to make offers for lease options and seller financing. When they saw me, most of them looked at me like, "Who are you and what are doing here?"

I was nineteen, but I looked like I was fifteen. At the time, I was only five feet seven and weighed about 130 pounds when wet. I still hadn't gone through puberty, my voice hadn't changed, and I had acne. To them, I just looked like some snot-nosed kid, so, obviously they all told me no. Clearly I didn't fit their image of a real estate, savvy tycoon.

Finally, I got a lead on a duplex from a Realtor I knew named, Arnie Woodard. He warned me that the owner was an ornery old guy who would likely turn me down immediately. I called him anyway. Arnie was right, the guy was an angry old cuss, and wouldn't take my offer.

But before I hung up, I happened to ask the magic question that I now tell all my students to ask, which was, "Do you have any other properties for sale?"

He said, "You know, now that you mention it, I'm the custodian for the estate of a friend of mine. She passed away and left a really dilapidated old house to her son, who is mentally handicapped. Now that she's gone, he needs to be in a facility, and I have to sell the house to pay for his care."

I heard myself say, "That sounds like something that would work for me." It was the first time I had a really good chance on getting a property. Anything sounded good!

Later that day I called Brent, the pharmacist, and told him about the deal. We scheduled a time to go and look at it.

When we got to the property, it was dusk. Brent and I poked around the house with flashlights, trying to get a sense of just how bad it was. The guy on the phone was right. The property was really beat up and the poor son had been living there alone with no electricity or running water for weeks, if not months. When we went into the basement, we found a puddle that looked like someone had spilled apple juice and the smell was horrible.

Turns out, because the water had been turned off, the son began urinating in five gallon buckets that he then stored on a shelf in the basement. The "apple juice" was actually urine. He had bowel movements in plastic bags, then tied them up and put them on the shelf next to the buckets. To make the situation more bizarre, we found the poor man hiding under the porch like "Boo Radley" from *To Kill a Mockingbird*.

It was both spooky and sad to see someone reduced to such squalor.

The asking price for the house was $60,000. I wrote an offer for $25,000 and they countered at $50,000. We finally settled at $35,000.

Being a realtor, Arnie had financial connections and he set me up with a private money lender, who Brent got a loan from. We then used his credit cards for materials.

The place was a mess. In the first six months we hauled away nine, fifteen-yard containers of garbage, debris, and human excrement out of the property. We had to rip out the kitchen and all of the bathroom and it took more money than we planned on using. Before long our finances were running really low.

That's when we found out that the whole house had lead pipes and needed to be re-plumbed. The plumber gave us a bid for $2,200, which at the time we didn't have. We were almost out of money. Luckily for us, the plumber had a creative financing streak – and looked around the property for any possible value. There was a beautiful antique upright piano still left in the house and he said, "Tell you what, give me that piano and I'll plumb the whole house for $500."

While the plumber worked on the pipes, we continued with the renovation. The old house was beginning to look great. The walls, the trim, the kitchen, and bathrooms were done. Everything was beautiful. The only thing left was to replace the carpet. But to do that, we had to move the piano.

When the plumber pulled up with his truck, we strapped the piano to his dolly and started to wheel it out. Everything was fine until we got to the door and realized we couldn't get the piano through it. The doorway was way too narrow. It was as if the entire house was built around that one piece of furniture. We had to take a sledgehammer and demo the wall we had just finished restoring and even after that, we couldn't turn it in the narrow hallway. We had to tear out the back of the bedroom closet and another wall to just get the piano out the front door. We had to spend another $800, which we didn't really have, to repair all the damage we created just to get the dang piano out of the door. It was a hard lesson to learn.

Eventually we sold the house for $79,000. We paid $35,000 and put $15,000 worth of materials into it, meaning we had $50,000 wrapped up in this first house. We re-invested the $29,000 profit into a duplex, which we fixed and flipped and then rolled that profit into a four-plex and twelve-plex, which we kept and rented out. At the tender age of twenty, things in the real estate space were really starting to take off.

But when I looked at the future, I didn't see myself being satisfied just fixing up and flipping houses. I wanted to find a different, more direct, and less labor-intensive pathway to wealth. I was searching for the kind of wealth they talked about at the real estate seminar.

About that time, I started reading Robert Kiyosaki's classic book, *Rich Dad, Poor Dad*. One of the principles goes something like this, "If you want to be rich and successful, you need to associate on a regular basis with rich and successful people."

The only rich, successful people I knew, at that time, were working for the seminar company. So I called the company and asked for a job.

Unfortunately, their policy was not to hire students. Not to be easily swayed, I asked to talk to the manager. I continued up the chain of command with the same response, "We don't hire students." Eventually, I worked my way up to Richard Brevoort, president of the company and the founder, Russ Whitney's, right hand man. After an impassioned 20 minutes speech about why I wanted to work there, what I could bring to the company, and what I wanted to learn, and after not taking no for an answer, he finally agreed to "think" about hiring me with two very big caveats attached. First I had to do ten real estate fix and flip deals and second I had to get two years sales experience under my belt.

While his response wasn't overwhelmingly optimistic, and I had some huge milestones to accomplish before he would even "think" about hiring me, I didn't let that trip me up. On my way to the grocery store that evening, I began taking inventory of my situation. There weren't any real sales jobs at the store, so I was going to need to widen my sphere of influence and look for a sales job elsewhere.

On my breaks, I scoured the newspaper for sales jobs. I found a lot of positions available, but there was nothing that I was qualified for. Everyone wanted a college degree, experience, and a sizeable resume. I didn't have the degree or experience, so I paid a professional company $400 to write a resume for me.

When I came across an ad for a territory sales representative for Keystone Packaging, I gathered up my courage and sent in my resume. Not long after that, I got an interview with the president of the company. Although my investment in a professionally written resume got me the interview, I now had my first opportunity to sell myself.

The president, Harvey Singleton, brought me into a conference room and wasted no time asking me a lot of hard questions. Eventually he raked me over the coals for wasting his time with my inexperience in the field. Over the next two weeks I didn't receive a letter or a call back regarding the job.

So I gathered up my courage again and I called the company and asked the receptionist if the position was still available. She said they were still looking and basically gave me the, "Don't call us, we'll call you" line.

I didn't take her advice. For the next several weeks, three times a week – Monday, Wednesday and Friday – I called and asked for Harvey. Each time I was told that he was in a meeting and unable to talk. This went on for about three months before Harvey gave me a second interview. Again I was unable to convince him to hire me, so I ratcheted up the calls to five times a week – Monday through Friday – until he finally cracked and brought me in for a third interview.

He said, "Lee, before I give you a job, you need to know that I don't think you can sell and be successful at this job. To be honest, the territory that I'm giving you currently has no customers or business. The only reason I'm even considering doing this is so you'll stop bugging me!"

I didn't care. I had my first sales job and I was that much closer to getting my job with the seminar company. Now I just had to take a territory that had no customers and zero sales and do something with it.

I had numerous chances to back off, back down, and quit. But the same tenacity that got me to that place in my life, kept me from stopping. I saw no option to give up. I could only keep moving forward.

PART 1
EXECUTING THE STRATEGY

Now that you have many pieces of The Circle in place, it's time to start building. This is what all the entrepreneurial racehorses out there have been waiting for. They've been chomping at the bit to start doing something. Well, now is the time. The bell is ringing and the gates are open, so go!

On your journey toward success, it will be critical for you to stay motivated. A tangible deliverable is something that needs to be done, and a date by which it has to be accomplished. Those two elements can act as motivational triggers.

It's not always possible to immediately convert an idea into cash. Often there is a time period between the conception of an idea, the execution, and the actual success. It requires time and patience to lay the proper foundation, and then time for that foundation to take hold and bear fruit.

So, how do you know if your strategy is paying off?

Money is a pretty good barometer of business success. The acquisition of wealth provides literal proof that your planning and actions can translate into dollars and cents. If you're making money, it's working; if you're not making money, it's not. Simple as that.

One of my associates has shortened the concept into five words, "Up and to the right." It refers to a graph that's showing favorable growth –

moving up and to the right. This is what everyone in the business world wants to see.

It's wise to set benchmarks to know that your business is heading in the right direction. But, "up and to the right" doesn't have to refer only to finances. It can also refer to streamlining your systems? Are you making more money with less effort? Are you making money quicker? Are you refining your vision? Are you enlarging your sphere of influence? Those are other ways to move up and to the right, but with less tangible financial benchmarks.

The question to ask is, "Am I on the right course to take me from where I am to where I want to be?" And it's wise to ask this question often.

♦ ♦ ♦

In business, it's important to understand the profit motive. Get this cemented in your thinking – you're in business to make a profit. The formula is, if you want X from me, pay me Y and I will deliver. You're not in it for any other reason. If you are, what you really have is a hobby or a non-profit organization. There's nothing wrong with either of those pursuits, but this book is not about that. It's about doing business with making a profit as the end goal.

My brother-in-law is a classic example of not understanding the profit motive. In 2006, before the bottom dropped out of the real estate market, my brother-in-law was a homebuilder in Salt Lake City. Business was good and he had plenty of customers. However, he was in the habit of spending a lot of time doing free consultations. He would go out to a prospective client's property, look over their building plans, and advise them at no cost.

I asked him why he wasn't charging for such a valuable service. He shrugged and said, "None of my competitors are charging for consultations, so people don't expect to pay for it."

I asked, "Are those really the kind of clients you want? Clients who expect you to work for free? If they get that for free, guaranteed they'll expect other services for free too. Why are you running your business like a non-profit? I personally wouldn't hire a contractor who thought his time was worthless."

My brother-in-law was so offended by that conversation that he still brings it up to this day. But guess what? He's no longer in construction.

He had to file for bankruptcy because he didn't run his business like a business.

That said, the costs of doing business can seem prohibitive and the competition can be fierce. Therefore, it's imperative that you understand how to make a profit. It's also important to know how and when to reinvest in your company. People often think they have to continually reinvest their profit back into their company and they get ahead of themselves. They try to force expansion, rather than allow the business to expand organically. They get so bogged down with all the imaginary preliminaries that they forget about the whole point – which is to make money. It is best to only invest the minimum amount necessary back into your business so that you're still earning a profit.

For example: a couple I consulted with told me that they had formed two LLCs. I said, "Wow, that's great. You're really growing." They then said that they spent $6,000 in legal fees getting it all set up. I said, "Fantastic. You must be making a nice profit." They kind of shuffled around and said, "Actually, we haven't made any money yet. We're just getting started. Our attorney said…"

That's when I cut them off. "What? You spent $6,000 on attorney fees to set up your corporations and you haven't even started making money yet? At this rate your attorney is making a tidy sum, but you're hemorrhaging cash!"

The best opinion I can give, and it's just that – an opinion, so don't construe this as legal advice – is to not form an LLC, a corporation, or worry about being an S-Corp, a C-Corp, or a partnership until your business has made at least $10,000 in revenue. Whether you mow lawns or you have a lemonade stand, until you've made somewhere in the neighborhood of $10,000 do you have enough assets to warrant the cost of trying to protect them, i.e. through the creation of a legal entity. Once you have made $10,000, there are online companies that will allow you to create the articles of incorporation for only $99, plus the fees for your state.

At this point in your business you should also start spending time each week taking inventory. I would ask myself if what I'm doing is actually making money, or at least has the potential to make money. I would ask, "What did I do this week that produced revenue? What opportunities did I explore? What relationships did I create or further that could produce revenue in the future?" Then, I would think about those same points in the negative. "What did I do that didn't produce revenue? What opportunities did I miss? What profitable relationships have I let slip? What relationships should I let go?"

Also, don't be too quick to expand. You should have a firm foundation before you head into an expansion. Businesses don't operate in a vacuum and you should use all available information and indicators to time your expansion for the greatest possible advantage.

Profit is the product of sound decisions. As I said, it's an indication of a sound strategy. You may need to fine-tune your approach from time to time, but if you're making money, at least you know you're heading in the right direction.

♦ ♦ ♦

Entrepreneurs are wise to understand when and why to hire employees. It's imperative to know when, and in what capacity, to bring people into your organization, especially in positions of influence.

My wife's grandfather had a great saying. It goes like this, "One man. Two men. Three men." Meaning, one person has the intelligence of one individual. But two people collaborating have the intelligence of three individuals. You have what the first person knows, and what the second person knows, plus you have what their knowledge combined produces, which often yields outstanding results.

But the analogy doesn't stop there.

It continues, "Three men. Two men. Four men. One." Meaning, when three people collaborate, they will often end up in opposition. It's no longer a collaboration. Usually you'll have two siding against one. So, you get the results of two individuals without any of the benefits of collaboration. If you add a fourth person to the mix, the conflict intensifies. Often it's two against two, canceling each other out, and sending you back to the results of one, single individual.

When I was fixing houses, I eventually realized it was best to hire a two-man crew. At one time I thought I could speed things up by hiring a larger crew. However, every time I tried to add a third or fourth man, the over-all productivity would drop. Instead of two guys supporting each other to get the job done as quickly as possible, you had other opinions, other views, and other techniques from the third and fourth individual which would bog down the communication and the process as a whole.

♦ ♦ ♦

There are a multitude of questions you need to answer before you hire anyone. You need to know why you're hiring, when to hire, how to hire, and who to hire.

Ask yourself – what is it I need the employee to do? Can I do it myself or can someone else do it better or faster than I can? Can I afford to pay someone to do it for me? Is the improvement they will make worth the cost? Will I have time to monitor the new employee's work? Do I know what I'm looking for in an employee? Can I interview prospective employees effectively? Will I know how to find the information I'm looking for on a candidate's resume? Can I evaluate a candidate's character just by talking to them? Do I have a benchmark to evaluate which candidate is best for the job?

Another way to tell if it's time to hire someone is if they can do the job more inexpensively than you can. To know that, you first have to place an actual numeric value on your time. To make it easy, let's say you've decided your time is worth $50 per hour and you're wondering if you should hire someone to clean your house. If housekeeping services are about $20 per hour, than it's obviously cheaper to hire someone else to clean your house.

♦ ♦ ♦

Employees are expensive. Have you ever heard of an employee paying his or her own way to attend a seminar? Or have you ever heard of an employee joining a business webinar and not getting paid for it? Or have you ever heard of an employee hiring a consultant to advise them how to improve their productivity?

If people would be willing to invest in improving their productivity, more money would be easier to come by, making them an asset. Companies will pay more for an asset than they will for an employee.

Unfortunately, most employees will never take the leap of logic to think about where they fit into the company's bottom line or how they can increase the value they bring to the company. Some people have the mistaken notion that because they've sat in their office chair longer than anyone else in the department, they deserve a higher wage. Unfortunately, common business practice has reinforced that notion. I'm here to tell you that notion is wrong.

The real reason an employee should make more than anyone else in the department is because he or she is more valuable to the organization. A higher wage can be expected year after year, when an employee consistently helps create more revenue for the company and the company can't afford to lose him or her.

Most employees don't think like that. Many believe that their employer should pay for things like seminars, webinars, or consultants. This illustrates the very real reasons a business owner should answer all the questions I mentioned before when taking on an employee. Know who you're hiring and why, and most importantly what their goals and motivations are for success and wealth. The go-getters and self-starters are out there but they are far and few between. Being discerning in your hiring practice will help you find them.

♦ ♦ ♦

It's time to address the fear of executing your strategy. For the most part, you will just have to ignore it and keep moving forward.

For example, when I decided I wanted to be a public speaker, I immediately came up against the roadblock of stage fright. If I wanted to accomplish my goal, I would need to come up with some kind of strategy and I would have to execute it to the best of my ability.

My first step was to start reading books about speaking and the first book I picked up was *Public Speaking for Dummies*. They addressed that stage fright and a fear of public speaking are basically fears of the unknown. One way to combat these fears is to get to know the space you'll be speaking in. They suggest going to the room beforehand to familiarize yourself with the environment. Is there a stage, a podium, or a lectern? How high is the stage? How many chairs are in the room? How close are the rows? When you stand on the stage, actually visualize speaking to a room filled with people. This simple task goes a long way to conquering the fear of speaking.

So, how do you overcome fear? The answer is: eliminate the unknowns as much as possible.

Overcoming fear of taking action can be as simple as researching the concerns you have about something. Going into something without any sense of what you're getting into is like playing a game of cards, and trying to decide whether to bet without seeing what you have in your hand. By looking at your cards, you'll know when you should bet, and how much, and that takes the fear away.

♦ ♦ ♦

On your road to success, a set-back may be the best thing that can happen to you even though it may not seem like it at the time. That's why I tell my students failure is good for you. Of course you won't enjoy it, but you can learn a great deal from failure. A willingness to learn from your mistakes can turn set-backs into stepping-stones to success.

Because understanding a problem is the first step to finding an answer, make up your mind to learn from your experiences, both positive and negative. Success isn't about knowing all the answers, but knowing how to find them. A successful person is a resourceful person. The person I'm most interested in working with is the person who says, "I don't know all the answers yet, but I know I can find them." That is much better than the person that says, "Get out of my way because I already know what I'm doing."

In the second scenario, you are only as capable, informed, and knowledgeable as you are right now. That's it. If you don't allow for the collaboration with other intelligent people, or you're not willing to read and expand your knowledge, then you will only ever be as good as you are presently. You'll only be able to go as high as you've ever been and that's very limiting.

♦ ♦ ♦

It's also important to learn to think on your feet. Sometimes you don't have half a day to mull something over. As I said before, if you don't have an answer to something, you need to learn how to find it. If someone else has to do all the heavy lifting to find the solution to a problem, you've learned nothing. If you don't learn to tackle problems, you'll never know what problem solving skills you're missing and you'll never know that those skills are missing until you need them. Learning to figure out things for myself has been just as important to my success as learning how to work was.

I tell this to the students at my seminars and to all my employees.

Recently my receptionist called saying, "Lee, how do you _____?"

I don't even remember what she wanted.

I asked, "How old are you?"

"Nineteen," she replied.

I said, "Then you're old enough to figure it out."

If I always tell her what to do and how to do it, she learns nothing. That's not to say I never help her, my other employees, or my students. I do. I just won't help them until they've put in some effort to figure it out for themselves.

◆ ◆ ◆

Any given task will expand to fill the time allotted. It's a rarely understood truth.

Everyone gets twenty-four hours a day, seven days a week. Using, "I don't have enough time," as an excuse is ridiculous. You have the same amount as everyone else. The point is, to be successful you will need to learn to maximize your time. This is crucial when executing a strategy.

Time is finite. It can't be replenished. Once it's spent, you can't get it back. I've made millions of dollars, lost it all, and made it back again and then some. But I've lost thousands of minutes that I will never be able to spend again, no matter what I do. It's the same for you.

In my career, I've written the curriculum for several real estate courses and a book. When I'm finished, this will be my second book. This may sound like I've accomplished a lot, but there are entrepreneurs out there who write a book every year. How do they run multi-million dollar organizations, have the same amount of time as I do, and write a book each year? Even though I ask the question, I already know the answer.

The truth is, they choose to use their time differently than I do. They opt to devote more time to writing. I haven't chosen to allocate as many hours to that as they have. Those entrepreneurs are choosing to use their time toward an end goal that's different than mine.

There isn't anything wrong with that. I have every right to choose different priorities and everything is fine as long as I don't start whining and saying, "I want to write a book a year too, but I can't because _____."

You get a better sense of the importance of how you allocate your time if you substitute the word "invest" to describe the use of time. What you choose to "invest" your time in will carry greater weight if you do this. Change your vocabulary from, "I don't have time for that." To, "I don't choose to invest my time in that." If you've been wasting time, it won't take long for you to start making changes in what you do with your greatest asset.

When you spend time with people, you're actually investing time in them. The question is, are you getting a good return on your investment? I'm sure you know people who, if given the chance, will waste your time. Just get on the phone with someone who's a talker and you can be there for hours without actually saying anything important or learning anything of value.

With the knowledge that time is a non-renewable resource, shouldn't you look for a return on every second you invest? Am I getting a good return? What does a tangible return on a time investment look like? Everyone should ask themselves those questions. If you aren't happy with the way your time balance-sheet looks, the only thing you can do is re-allocate the time you have into more positive ventures.

Try getting up an hour earlier. Read books about wealth creation, positive thinking, and success. After twenty-one days re-evaluate your life. Do you think more positively? Do you speak more positively? Are your relationships better? Are you doing better at work? Are you generating more income? Any of those would be a tangible return on the hours you chose to invest. Now you have to ask yourself, "Which do I prefer, the extra hours of sleep, or the improvements in the other areas of my life?"

The next thing to think about is work. Most people invest somewhere in the neighborhood of forty hours a week on their job. The return on investment is a paycheck. You trade your time for money. Are you getting the best possible return for those hours? Is there any way to invest the same forty hours and get a better return?

I also trade my time for money. The difference between the average worker and me is that I refuse to sell my time cheaply. The average worker makes $50,000 a year. I charge $50,000 a day.

I understand that people can't start where I am, but people should understand that I started where they are. In fact, I started at such a low wage that it's not even legal to pay people that anymore. I was trading an hour of my most precious asset for $3.90. If that was how low on the totem pole I was when I started working and we can see where I am today, just think where you could be with the right investment of time and the right type of work. No matter where you are today, you can make those adjustments to achieve a better return on investment in both your time and career. If you choose correctly, it shouldn't impact your security either.

◆ ◆ ◆

That's something everyone should think about. Is the illusion of security really worth the time you're giving in exchange?

People don't talk about this much, but a lot of what they think is giving them security is really an illusion. I don't have to think very hard to come up with examples. The company they work for could go out of business, or it could be part of a merger, eliminating their position. If there is a downturn, they could be laid off. In all these very real and common scenarios, there goes their health insurance and retirement. Their "solid" security often rests on a house of cards.

In essence, when you stay in a low-paying job only for the benefits, you're saying, "I don't want to take on the responsibility of setting up my own retirement plan or finding my own health insurance."

So, what's the answer? In my opinion, you do whatever you need to do to take as much control of your life as possible. In order to do this, it's imperative that you ask yourself if what you're doing is the most productive way to invest your time. If you want to change your life, you're going to have to change how you invest your time and then take responsibility for it. Simple as that.

No one wants to hear that they've been mismanaging their greatest asset. If you want to look deeper, your income speaks to how well you've spent your time. Your income is nothing more than the end result of how well you've invested your greatest asset.

51.4 Degrees of
Executing the Strategy

1. Take control by taking responsibility in your life.
2. Learn time management.
3. Understand your profit motive.
4. Overcome your challenges.
5. What are you doing to move up and to the right?
6. What is your sequence of implementing strategies?
7. How do you tell if a strategy is paying off?
8. Only invest time in the right people.
9. Don't sell your time too cheap for a false sense of security.

WHAT IS YOUR CURRENT VALUE OF TIME? DIVIDE INCOME EARNED BY HOURS WORKED. THIS BECOMES YOUR BASELINE. IF YOUR BASELINE IS $20/HR TO DO A TASK, THEN HIRE SOMEONE ELSE IF THEY CAN DO IT CHEAPER. IF IT COSTS MORE THAN $20/HR TO DO THE TASK, DO IT YOURSELF.

YOU SHOULD TAKE A BASELINE INVENTORY EVERY 6, 12, AND 18 MONTHS. IF YOU ARE SUCCESSFUL, YOUR TIME SHOULD BE MORE VALUABLE AS TIME GOES ON.

WHAT ARE YOUR TWO CORE COMPETENCIES OR MAIN STRENGTHS THAT ARE STRATEGIC ADVANTAGES?

1. _____   2. _____

PART 2
MY VENTURE

W hen my two-year anniversary with the packaging company came up, my territory, which had zero sales and zero customers when I first started, was the top-producing region in the company.

I believe what made me successful with that territory, where others had failed, was the fact that I had a larger goal driving me. As satisfying as it was to turn a failing region around, it was never my goal to make a career of being a regional sales rep. My goal was to satisfy Richard Brevoort, president of Russ Whitney's group, by getting two years of sales experience. The job at the packaging company was only a means to an end.

So, with two years of sales experience to the day and ten fix and flip real estate deals under my belt, I called Richard Brevoort.

When I told him who I was, his response was, "Who?"

"Lee Arnold. I've spent the past two years in regional sales. I turned a territory with zero customers and zero sales into the top-producing region for the company. I've been on the road fifty weeks a year and I've been making at least a hundred phone calls a week, and –"

He cut me off. "Who is this? Do we know each other?"

I was stunned, but tried not to sound like it. "Yes. If you recall, two years ago you told me to get two years of sales experience, and flip ten houses, which I've done and – "

He cut me off again. "Why did you do that?"

"So I could come work for you."

"Whoa, whoa, whoa. Hold on a minute. Did I say I would hire you?"

"Yes, that's what you said. After I attended one of your seminars, I called you for a job."

"But we have a policy that we don't hire our students."

It was deja vu. Two years had passed and we were having the exact same conversation. I responded, "I know, however you said if I got two years sales experience and did ten fix and flips, you'd make an exception. I have done this."

There was a long silence.

Richard finally said, "Okay, tell you what. We have a convention next week in Cape Coral, Florida. If you buy a ticket and get down there, I'll make sure you get an interview."

My confidence was deflated. I went from expecting a job outright to simply getting an interview. I bought an airline ticket, anyway, and paid $1000 to get into the event.

When I went into the hotel conference room, Russ Whitney himself was onstage. There were 400 people in the room and for three hours, nobody moved. They, and I, were spellbound, hanging onto every word he said. He had all of us in the palm of his hand. I remember thinking, "I want to be just like him. I want to speak, influence, and help people too."

True to his word, Richard made sure I had an interview with Russ Whitney's daughter, Thea. During the interview, she asked, "So, Lee, why do you want to work for us?"

I said, "I really respect what Russ has done. I love that your company helps people and I want to be part of it. I want to glean everything I can from him." About five hours later, someone came and told me that I had a job, and I would start in two weeks.

Now, I had a whole new problem. The job was in Cape Coral, Florida but I lived in Spokane, Washington. I had never lived outside of the Northwest and here I was moving to the other side of the country.

I had to quit my job, close all my accounts, figure out what to do with my investment properties, pack my stuff up, sell what I wasn't taking, and be back in Cape Coral in just two weeks.

In my favor, I had three things to motivate me. A tangible deliverable – something that had to be done, a date by which it had to be accomplished and a motivational trigger, the pleasure of getting the job I wanted.

First, I had to tell my parents though. The response was predictable. "You're doing what?" Eventually, they warmed up to the idea, probably because there wasn't anything they could do about it. Next, I had to settle all my businesses and accounts, pack the stuff I was taking with me, and sell the stuff I wasn't. Everything I was bringing fit in the back of my truck, which, ironically, if you remember, I had previously refinanced to get the money to go to that first real estate seminar. Now I was driving to Florida in it to work for that same company.

I bought new wheels and tires for the 3,200 mile journey, drove cross-country to settle in Cape Coral, Florida, and I went to work for the seminar company. I couldn't believe it. I was working for Russ Whitney, the guy who kept 400 people spellbound for three hours!

Monday mornings I went to the corporate office with the sales reps for sales training with Russ. Then, at 2:00 PM a cab took the four of us, who were on the road crew, to the airport, and we flew to the location of the next seminar. We would put on a sales seminar, the same exact one that hooked me several years previously, on Tuesday at 1:00 PM and then another one at 6:00 PM. We would then pack up all our equipment, load up our bags, and drive thirty to forty miles to the next location. We would repeat the process – setting everything up to do a seminar at 1:00 PM and another at 6:00 PM, tear it all down and drive to the next hotel – on Wednesday and Thursday. Then on Thursday night, we would let loose, go out, and drink way too much. On Friday, we would get up early and fly back to Florida. On Saturday, I would hit the laundromat to wash my clothes for the next week and on Sunday, I would spend the day catching up on my much needed sleep. When Monday hit, we'd do it all over again.

Over time, my dream job wasn't exactly what I had thought it was going to be. My life was go, go, go... all of the time. There were mornings I woke up and had to look at a motel room phonebook just to see where I was. I had been to almost every city in the United States, but never really experienced any of them. I only saw the insides of motel rooms and hotel ballrooms and pretty soon, they all looked the same.

In 2000, Russ Whitney formed Whitney Mortgage, which was run by a guy named Dave Heaps. In July of that year, we were putting on a seminar in Salt Lake City at the downtown Sheraton. Dave was in the back of the hotel ballroom with his wife, Valerie.

She told us how she wanted us to meet her little sister who lived in Salt Lake and who had just broken off an engagement a few months earlier. We were all single guys and never turned down the chance to meet a pretty girl. When Jaclyn walked into the room, all of us on the road crew called "dibs." She was beautiful. Since we all called "dibs" on her, it became a "may the best man win" scenario. I took the initiative and pulled her aside first. I asked her to have dinner and dancing with me after the seminar was over.

Her response was a resounding, "No."

I used my life-lessons of persistence and determination and doggedly continued to try to woo her until she finally cracked and said she would only go out with me if I was a Pisces.

I said, "That'll work." I showed her my driver's license, which proved I was born March 15th and therefore she had to go out with me. Just as I predicted, we had a great time and we soon started a long-distance relationship.

Because Jaclyn lived in Salt Lake City, I eventually transferred to a subsidiary company, Whitney Consulting, located in Salt Lake City in November of 2000. They gave me the option of being in telephone sales or consulting. Sales sold the big-ticket coaching packages that the consultants fulfilled. I had already been on the sales side and wanted to learn the "helping" side of the business too, so I chose consulting.

At the time I was twenty-three and although I had achieved my goal to work for the seminar company, and it was probably the most dynamic thing I could have done at the time, I still didn't feel fulfilled. I wanted more. I wanted to be a public speaker, like Russ Whitney, and captivate and educate a roomful of people. I felt like that was my ultimate and true purpose in life.

Once I made up my mind that I wanted to speak, I bought every book I could find on speaking and communication. I read *Public Speaking for*

Dummies and *Public Speaking for Success*, by Dale Carnegie. I also enrolled in Dale Carnegie's twelve-week course on *How to Win Friends and Influence People*.

I took any opportunity I had to speak in front of an audience. I even told Russ that I would like to speak for the company. Unfortunately, they preferred to keep me on the phone, wearing a head-set, and consulting for them instead.

To keep from being discouraged, I bought a poster of an audience and hung it in my office. While I was on the phone, I imagined myself talking to that audience. I'd make eye-contact with the guy in back, the lady in the aisle seat, or the older couple in the front row. Eventually I got comfortable speaking to the people in the poster.

Just like all the other times in my life when I hit a brick wall, I began looking for a way to achieve my goal. Just as before, I knew I could only keep going forward and that, eventually, I would figure it out.

CHAPTER SIX

PART 1
BECOMING THE ENTREPRENEUR

arts 1 through 5 of The Circle of Wealth are where you cut your teeth and earn your chops. Now you are coming to the place of making money without working for it and, where once you were taking from The Circle, now you're in the position to help those who are starting their journey. You now have the ability to offer them your knowledge and capital.

You can look around The Circle for someone who has an opportunity and needs an investor. You provide the capital while they do all the leg work of executing the plan and assembling the power team to get the job done.

Most of us have been trained that we should get up Monday through Friday, or some version of that, and go to work. Few of us, however, have been taught that money can work for us. Now it's time for your money to start going to work for you.

A statement I made in Part 1 bears repeating here: if you're working for money, it's the worst boss you'll ever have. However, if money is working for you, it's the best employee you'll ever hire. In The Circle of Wealth, borrowers typically send lenders a check every month, as an interest-only payment, an interest plus principle payment, or a compounding interest payment on the loan. It's called passive income and it's a great place to be. When you have several sources of passive income coming in, you can begin to rapidly amass wealth because money invested works around the clock.

♦ ♦ ♦

Making money work for you takes a bit of thought and planning though.

Let me explain. Let's say, like me, you've been buying and selling real estate and you made $15,000 on your last fix and flip, which means you're now in the position that you need to do it again. You're back where you started. This is called being in the buy, fix, sell; buy, fix, sell; buy, fix, sell cycle. In this scenario there is no continuity of income and no ongoing revenue source.

Now you could take your $15,000 profit and use it as a down payment on another house, or you could loan the money to someone else at 10% interest, which would give you an extra $1,500 a year. That's nice, but it's not really enough do a whole lot with.

You could also use your $15,000 as a down payment on a duplex, which has a mortgage payment of $1,000 a month. If your two tenants are each paying $750 in rent, you're making an extra $500 more than the mortgage. In a year's time, you would make $6,000. That's called continuity of income. If you repeat the process, you can see that, over time, you could make enough continuous income to live on.

On the flip-side, continual income often comes with what investors call "tail." Tail is the ongoing maintenance, management, and responsibility of an investment. In the duplex scenario, let's say you don't want to deal with maintaining the property and collecting rent any longer, so you hire a property manager who charges $300 a month for their services. At this point you're now only making $200 a month. The "tail" is eating up more than half your profit.

Now the idea isn't to do either/or on any of this. The wise choice is to do a little of all the above and then put your profits into a self-directed IRA. That way you can limit inflation and taxes. The idea with investing is to make as much and keep as much as you can. If you make post-tax contributions, you won't have to pay a cent of tax when you start making withdrawals. Every dollar you earn in that type of IRA is tax-free.

♦ ♦ ♦

As an investor, you should have two questions for a prospective borrower in The Circle of Wealth. "What's the yield on my investment? What's the return?" The yield refers to how much interest they will pay you and the return refers to how you will actually be repaid the debt. It could be said this way, "If I invest $1 million, how much am I going to make on the deal and how are you going to pay me back?"

◆ ◆ ◆

In real estate investment terms, in this part of The Circle, you are in a position where you no longer have to find the property, write the offer, hang the sheetrock, paint the walls, re-do the kitchen, and sell the property yourself. As a lender, you provide the financing and your borrower does all the work. If I'm the lender, I'll want to know the price point to loan value of the property and the upside market timing. As a lender, besides the qualifications of the borrowers, I need to decide whether I'm going to lend through a checking account, an IRA, or a 401k.

At the beginning stages of this part of The Circle of Wealth journey, you'll be using your own money and it's wise to be dealing with smaller, short-term loans. It's not abnormal or imprudent to be risk-averse or too careful with whom you loan your money to.

That said, in The Circle of Wealth, the mentality isn't one of hoarding and storing up. The idea is to send what you've earned and learned back into the marketplace and continue earning because of it. It's what we call a win/win. You're benefiting by earning a passive income and you're benefiting others because you're supplying capital to them. Under this model, there is an abundance of wealth available and you can make as much as you want. However, the moment you start hoarding and thinking, "This is mine and I need to hang on to it," your wealth will start to shrink. Essentially you've said, "This is all I'm going to get." You end up paralyzed and sitting on what you've earned.

Luke 12:18-21

> *...This is what I'll do. I will tear down my barns and build bigger ones, and there I will store my surplus grain. And I'll say to myself, You have plenty of grain laid up for many years. Take life easy; eat, drink and be merry. But God said to him, You fool! This very night your life will be demanded from you. Then who will get what you have prepared for yourself? This is how it will be with whoever stores up things for themselves but is not rich toward God. (NIV)*

◆ ◆ ◆

You may have heard the saying, "When there is blood in the streets –
buy." More money is made in a down economy than a good economy.
There is no way I could have built my company to its present size in a
thriving economy. Even as I'm writing this book, I'm actually concerned that the stock market is running too high. For every thousand
points the market goes up, it creates trillions of dollars in liquidity.
When there are trillions of dollars in flux, the market gets stupid. When
the market gets stupid, money flows to stupid people and when you put
money in the hands of stupid people, all sorts of insane things can happen. This is exactly what we saw in the markets before the 2008
meltdown.

At that time, smart investors sold when the market was at its peak and
made a tidy windfall. They saw the signs, liquidated, and then waited
until everything blew over.

Since 2008, people aren't spending and banks aren't lending – at least
not the way they used to before the meltdown. Stupid money dried up,
and stupid people pulled back on their investments. That left an opening
for smart investors to jump back into the game. Fortunately, my company is all about taking smart money and lending it to smart people. So,
as the rest of the financial world was imploding, we were lending and
expanding.

If you're an experienced investor and you closely follow the market,
you know that it cycles about every ten years. Investing shouldn't be
based entirely on the economy; you should also consider where the market is likely to be in the cycle.

It's also important to understand that, like the market, businesses have
a life cycle too. If a business is successful, it's alive and its rate of
growth is tied to its overall health. Yet, when a business model becomes
outdated (which they often do), you need to change its lifespan by expansion, diversification, or reorganization. The thing to remember is
that the time will come when you will need to do something to revive
your business model.

Some entrepreneurs try to take the simple route by putting their aged,
dying business on life support. They try to give it a transfusion – or an
infusion of cash. But cash alone can't fix a life cycle problem. Throwing
money at a business model that has run its course is only prolonging the
inevitable. Even businesses that have been around for years, change the
way they operate as times change. If they don't, they will become part

of history. There are always aggressive, up-and-coming competitors looking to take the place of an established business. Be aware that dwindling growth is a sign of a business model that needs an overhaul.

♦ ♦ ♦

One of the fastest ways to move ahead is to always ask if there is anything more. Is there anything else I can do? Is there anything more you can teach me or that I can teach you? Is there another opportunity or another way of looking at an opportunity? That said, no matter what your financial picture is, to be truly successful, you need to start giving.

Someone in the first parts of The Circle might say, "But, Lee, I'm only making $35,000 a year and I'm already struggling."

I reply, "Well, then let's take a look at your budget and see what we can do."

If you don't know your budget, it's impossible not to struggle.

Then I ask, "How about taxes? Let me see your returns."

It's surprising how many people don't file their taxes. Even the Bible says to render to Caesar what is Caesar's.

Mark 12:17

> Then Jesus said to them, "Give back to Caesar [taxes] what is Caesar's and to God what is God's." And they were amazed at him. (NIV)

Religious or not, these are foundational principles. Clearly, you aren't being a good steward of what you have, so why would anyone trust you with more?

Admittedly, the lower your income, the harder life is. When you're flat broke, everything is a crisis because money is tight and there's no surplus. Yet, if you came to me, I would show you how simple it is to carve out 10% of your income for giving, which the Bible calls a "tithe." For this example, I'll use the slightly-below average income of $40,000 a year. Ten percent of that is $4,000, which would be about $320 a month.

The first thing I would cut is cable TV. Depending on your cable package that could be the whole $320. The average American watches thirty-three hours of television a week. If you could find a job making $10 an hour, and worked during those TV hours, you could make an extra $330 a month. That would be close to $4,000 a year, which would almost pay for all of your giving.

While the decision to take money from your budget for giving is a simple one, it's not an easy one to do. As I said before, if it was easy everyone would be doing it. As I'll explain in the next chapter, the rewards are well worth the effort though.

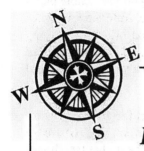

51.4 Degrees of

Becoming an Independent Entrepreneur/Investor

1. Let money work for you.
2. Learn the continuity of income.
3. What investments do you have that have "tail?"
4. Learn to keep as much profit as possible.
5. Buy in a down market.
6. Limit your inflation and taxes.
7. Get rid of the idea of hoarding and storing up.
8. Start to give back.

WHAT PERCENTAGE OF YOUR INCOME IS PASSIVE AND WHAT PERCENTAGE IS EARNED?

_____% PASSIVE   _____% EARNED

HOW MUCH MONEY HAVE YOU MADE $_____

HOW MUCH MONEY HAVE YOU SPENT $_____

TOTAL INCOME YOU HAVE SAVED _____%

TOTAL INCOME YOU HAVE TITHED _____%

HOW WOULD YOU LIKE TO SEE THESE PERCENTAGES AND AMOUNTS CHANGE IN THE NEXT SIX MONTHS?

MONEY MADE $_____   INCOME SAVED _____%

MONEY SPENT $_____   INCOME TITHED _____%

PART 2
MY VENTURE

PART 2
MY VENTURE

By the time 2002 rolled around, I was twenty-five and Russ Whitney and I had parted ways amicably. I wanted more room to grow and develop as a speaker, teacher, and mentor, so I set out to find success on my own. I have always been grateful for what I learned at Russ Whitney's company and for the dreams that were ignited that fateful night when I flipped the channel to his infomercial.

That year, I got my real estate license and I went back to investing and, most importantly, I married Jaclyn.

Early in 2003, I had one of the biggest, bitter/sweet ah-ha moments of my career. I had the opportunity to partner with a real estate conglomerate in Seattle called The Foreclosure Group. They bought and sold ten to fifteen foreclosure houses a week at auction, and made around $3 million a year.

They asked me to set up a satellite office in Salt Lake City, using their business model. It wasn't long before I noticed that we were making more money in pre-foreclosure short-sales than we were making at the auction. So they requested that I write a curriculum on short-selling and they would pay me a royalty of five percent from each sale. We called it *Endless Wealth*. They did all the marketing for it and in four months we made $1.8 million on it, which means my take was around $90,000. I was only twenty-six and I made $90,000 in four months. It was pretty heady stuff.

Although the internet was still fairly new back then, it didn't take long before I started to come across negative comments about me and the *Endless Wealth* curriculum. It mostly had to do with the poor customer service and empty promises made in the marketing to get people to buy the course. I called the company and said if they didn't get this under control, I would pull the curriculum. Because they held the keys to the kingdom – the customers – they said, "Go ahead. Pull the plug. The minute you do, we'll stop marketing and selling it." They were more concerned about the profit than my reputation.

The experience was a huge learning moment. Although, we didn't end on the best footing, I learned how to create educational materials and more importantly, I learned that he who controls the leads, controls everything.

I decided from that moment on, I would never allow myself to be in that position again. So, I broke away from The Foreclosure Group and started my own company. I have never again put myself in a situation where I had no direct contact with my customers. That's why some of my employees call me "The Lead Freak." When you have contact information for your customers, that's the beginning of a stream that can flow into a rushing waterfall of profit. It's also the only way you're going to develop a relationship of trust and loyalty with your clients.

In 2004 I hired a writer and co-wrote my own course called *Fortunes in Foreclosure*. I began speaking at my own seminars and selling my own products. What started out as a negative, turned out to be a great motivator toward something positive.

After breaking away from The Foreclosure Group, I partnered with a fellow in Texas and put on an event in Austin selling *Fortunes in Foreclosure*. We had that event four times each year in 2004, 2005, and 2006 and made about $1.5 million. That coupled with the other speaking engagements and all my real estate investments, I was making a tidy profit.

During this process, I learned to manage my business relationships better. I found that if I wanted to keep my reputation, I needed to keep tighter control on my interactions with clients. You can't do anything about something you aren't aware of, but the time to act, and confront if necessary, is the moment you realize there is something wrong.

In the case of the negative presence on the internet, I couldn't do anything until I knew about it. However, I should have taken control of how the foreclosure company handled my image from the start. I should have been more involved in where and how they marketed the product, and then monitored the results. I have learned that I can't let things unravel to the point of a toxic relationship, like what happened with The Foreclosure Group. This lesson has stayed with me since then.

While my professional career was skyrocketing, Jaclyn and I started our married life in a rented duplex, which I eventually bought. In our early years of marriage, like all newly married couples, we had dreams of owning our own home and starting our own family. On Sundays, after church, we would get a bucket of fried chicken and drive around the neighborhoods that we liked and wanted to live in.

The first neighborhood we wanted to settle down in was called Sugarhouse. Not only did we like the cute little bungalow homes, I also saw tremendous potential there. It was in a re-gentrification phase, with up-and-coming, eclectic shops and companies investing in the area and a young, more hip crowd gravitating to live there. After a few Sunday house-scouting drives, I found a bank-owned property two blocks from Sugarhouse Park and bought it for $120,000. The best part was, we were actually living in the neighborhood we had previously dreamed about.

As my professional career caught fire and my bank accounts reflected my success, our dreams got bigger and we started driving around an area of Salt Lake called Bell Canyon. These homes were much bigger, more elegant, and reflected better where I was at in my business and real estate career.

During this period, I happened to be at a real estate auction when a home in Bell Canyon came up for bidding. I broke a cardinal rule of real estate investing and bought the house site-unseen. I felt confident in the deal though since Jaclyn and I had been on so many Sunday recognizant missions prior to the auction. The house was built in 1997, had 6,800 square feet, and was on almost a full acre just six miles from a ski resort. The opening bid was $297,000 so I bid and bought it.

We sold the Sugarhouse property for $240,000, which meant that in two years we made a 100% return on that investment. By moving to Bell Canyon, once again we were living in a neighborhood we had both envisioned ourselves in. Although we loved the location, I'm not one to sit idle for very long and as we hit our two-year residence anniversary there, I started to dream bigger. We started driving to a new area called Steeplechase in the town of Draper, which is about twenty miles south of Salt Lake. At that time a lot of tech workers and entrepreneurs were buying in that area and I saw a huge profit potential there, like I had previously seen in Sugarhouse. Also, being involved in real estate, I spent a lot of time at the zoning and planning department and had the inside scoop on different areas throughout the Salt Lake valley. During that time period, I learned that the LDS church would be breaking ground on a new Mormon temple in the Steeplechase area. I had been in Salt Lake real estate long enough to know that wherever the LDS Church built a temple, property values skyrocketed.

Every Sunday after church and chicken, Jaclyn and I went to Draper and drove around Steeplechase. We found a property that had been on the market for a while. It was in good shape and the price was low, so I couldn't figure out why it hadn't sold. When I called the seller, I found out that she worked for eBay and had been transferred to Canada, which meant she had two mortgage payments. She was tired of going back and forth between the properties and was ready to get out from under it.

I asked her what she owed for the property, which at the time was $740,000, so that's what I offered her. She took the deal. We sold our property in Bell Canyon and made a $350,000 tax-free profit on it and then moved to Steeplechase.

A few days after we closed on the property, the LDS Church announced that they would be breaking ground on the new temple in three weeks. The Steeplechase property suddenly appraised for $1.3 million, which meant, in one fell swoop, I had $600,000 in equity on the house.

About that same time, I bought twenty lots for $400,000 and three weeks later the city re-zoned the density and my twenty lots became forty. I quickly flipped the lots for $800,000, and after fees and taxes, I made close to $400,000 on that one deal.

There were many transactions like that during that period of time. The world truly felt like my oyster. It felt like everything in the universe was conspiring to make me money. I was at the top of my game! Little ol' me from Spokane, Washington who made $3.90 an hour as a bag boy, was now a multi-millionaire at the young age of twenty-six. I had it all!

In 2004, the only dark cloud on my horizon was, that after years of try-ing, Jaclyn and I were unable to have children. We eventually went in for fertility treatments. It was then that I began to understand the true value of money. Because I had been successful in my business, I was able to afford the $28,000 it cost for us to have our twins, Aundreya Gene and Preston Larry.

The doctor cautioned us that once a couple conceives through treatment, many times it isn't too long before another baby is conceived naturally. Apparently, we didn't do a very good job heeding his warning because Harrison Theodore was born thirteen months later. We went from being childless to the parents of three almost overnight.

Suddenly every aspect of my life was in place. I had a beautiful wife and three healthy children. I owned eighty-five rental properties, a property management company, and my own seminar company. By all common measurements, I had achieved success.

PART 1
COMPLETING THE CIRCLE

Now you've achieved your goals. As an accredited investor, you have $1 million or more at your disposal and you have equity in your home. If you want (and why wouldn't you), you can take greater risks to reap greater rewards. You also have the capacity and the reputational, political, and financial capital to even go back through the other the parts of The Circle in another industry.

Most importantly, you're in a position to give back. Though it's been a long haul, it would be difficult, if not impossible, to achieve this level of success and maintain it if you hadn't gone through Parts 1 through 6.

In Part 7 you are in a position to dream larger and to be the person you always wanted to be. You have a wealth of experience under your belt and you're now able to imagine writing a sizeable check to a charity or mentoring someone else on their journey through The Circle.

When you reach the seventh part of The Circle of Wealth, you may ask, as many people who have reached their goals do, "Now that I'm here, what do I do next?"

That's an all-important question.

Having completed The Circle, you've reached your goal or goals. You've achieved what you planned and your life is full. You have money. You have investments and, for all intents and purposes, your life is secure. You have gained an understanding of the true riches in life: a happy home, a happy marriage, good health, great friendships, and/or wonderful, established working relationships.

This is when your motivation shifts to, "How many people can I help achieve their dreams? How can I give back and bless other people's lives?"

When you've reached this part of The Circle, you are in a position to bless those in Parts 1 through 6. You can reach back and help them to join you in Part 7. Why would you do this? So we can all pool our funds and create an even larger Circle of Wealth. We can bring in even more people which will increase our sphere of influence to feed the poor, help the homeless, or give to charity. The possibilities are endless to what we can do for others.

As someone who has completed The Circle, it's your job to go ahead of the others, hold the door open and say, "Come on in." You, and those who have achieved their goals, can then pool your resources to synergistically create an even greater ability to give back. You took what you needed to achieve success from The Circle with the awareness that, when you succeeded, you would have the desire to give back.

The whole point of life is to give. It's often an overlooked principle, but the awareness of the need to give back will help propel you to even greater success. The benefits of looking at life that way are well documented. Even people who seemingly have no reason to want to live, find purpose in life by giving back.

The Circle of Wealth provides opportunity, after opportunity, to not only to be blessed yourself, but to bless others. You learn to see opportunity in the light of helping others on their way up. It's no longer "how can I achieve my dream" but "how many people can I help to fulfill their goals and lofty ambitions."

♦ ♦ ♦

Some people who have a dream or a goal, don't have the resume or skill set to accomplish it. When they go looking for help – let's say for funding – they may be turned down because of what they're lacking, like credit or experience. If they get turned down often enough, they may quit altogether. It's the breaks that some of our biggest and brightest have received through The Circle of Wealth that has allowed them to achieve so much. In The Circle of Wealth, those who are the most successful would never allow other possible stars to never get their chance to shine. You need to give people something to strive for, some hope that they can be successful too.

Now you may be thinking, "How do I know if they are going to use my funds or knowledge to the best of their ability? How do I know they won't just fritter away these important resources? Remember before when I told you about calling for a job with Russ Whitney's company? They gave me two long-term goals to accomplish before they would even broach the conversation of employment with me. I do the same thing. When someone wants my financial or educational help, I often say, "Go do XYZ (the tasks are specific to the individual), and when you're done, contact me." I'm purposefully creating a roadblock, not to stop them, but to strengthen their resolve. I design the tasks to teach them a skill or skills they're lacking. It also shows how serious they are about achieving their goal. They need to know this because the road to success is hard and often filled with many trials and challenges.

When Richard Brevoort told me to go do 10 fix and flips and work in sales for two years, he was setting me up to not only be successful in Russ's company, but to be successful no matter what I did. It was one of the best things that someone could have done for me back then and I'm grateful for it.

Like Richard, I'm not interested in working with someone who has no tenacity. That's why I don't automatically take people under my wing. I need to know that they want what I have to offer more than I want to give it to them and that they want success for themselves more than I want it for them.

◆ ◆ ◆

Are you investing all your time, money and energy collecting stuff, or are you giving back? I'm not just talking about money. It's important to give of your time too, because as I said, it is your most precious resource. You may think you don't have any free time, but if you're like most of us, you could shave a few hours off and volunteer somewhere. If you did this, I guarantee you will witness a positive change in your life and be amazed at the transformation. You'll become more amiable and people will be drawn to you. You'll be more approachable, compassionate, and kind. In giving without any expectation of return, I guarantee that you will likely find the greatest opportunities present themselves. Who wouldn't rather do business with a kind, compassionate person?

If you want to move up in the world, I believe giving to others is the fastest way to do it. Why? Because once people see you as a value-add to their lives, you'll be an indispensable resource to them and that's a great and valuable position to be in.

Giving also makes you more successful. If you read biographies of successful entrepreneurs most of them have a habit of giving. Just look at Oprah, Bill Gates, Mark Zuckerberg, and Warren Buffet. Each one of these financial and influential greats have made huge contributions to society through financial donations towards social programs to help those who have much less than they do.

♦ ♦ ♦

As I said previously, Biblically speaking, 10% of your income is called a "tithe," meaning tenth. That's what many of the wealthiest entrepreneurs say they give – a tithe. But in the Bible, 10% is the minimum amount you should give. Giving the minimum certainly has benefits. But if you really want to see blessings come your way, give more. Try 20%. I know from experience, God will bless you in ways you can't even imagine, including financially.

♦ ♦ ♦

If you've read my story, you know what happened when I volunteered to serve Thanksgiving dinner to homeless people at the soup kitchen. That's not the only time that kind of thing happened as a result of giving.

While I charge a lot for a consultation, I also try to give back as a mentor. Once a month I do a free CEO Fireside Chat. I teach for 90 minutes or so and many of my best students, who have also become business partners, have come to me through this monthly educational service.

I recently flew to Dallas to speak at an event. I stayed several hours after the event, answering questions and consulting. During that time, I happened to run into a woman who is a heavy-hitter in the industry. I had heard about her for years, had read her books and promotional materials, but had never had the pleasure of meeting her. I introduced myself.

She said, "Lee Arnold? I've heard about you through the real estate grapevine."

We exchanged business cards and once home, I called her a few days later. I asked her the all-important question, "How can we make money together?" That's one of my favorite questions because it says that I don't want to take from you, instead, I want to work synergistically to make money together.

It turns out that soon she'll be speaking at one of my events and I'll be speaking at one of her events. I estimate that relationship will bring in an additional $50,000 to $100,000 in revenue, which only transpired from me spending a few hours giving back. It's funny, but it always seems to work out like that when you take the time to give.

◆ ◆ ◆

In my opinion, the most powerful business tool an entrepreneur has is prayer. It operates in a universal, spiritual sphere of influence we can't connect with on our own. That connection to God gives you access to a power greater than anyone can understand. The great thing is, the power of prayer isn't limited. Whether you need help with your business, your marriage, your children, or any other area of life, the power of prayer is available to you.

I can't imagine being an atheist entrepreneur. Who do you call on when things are spiraling out of control? Who do you call on when your feet are in the fire or your back is against the wall? What do you do when there is nothing else you can do? I'll tell you what I do, I pray.

It was my relationship with God that pulled me out of the swamp when the real estate bubble burst and I believe it is prayer that keeps my business afloat, my marriage happy, and my children healthy today.

◆ ◆ ◆

At church a while back, I ran into a man, who I'll call "Brian." I've known Brian for years but I hardly recognized him. We had kind of lost track of each other over the years; he went into the banking end of real estate, while I stayed in the investing.

He looked so broken that I couldn't help but ask him what happened. He had just been laid-off from his job at a bank because the bank was going through a merger. I was surprised because he was such a smart, responsible guy.

I asked, "Are you looking for work at the other banks? With all your experience it shouldn't be too hard to find something." He shook his head and said, "Lee, if I hadn't been laid off, I probably would have quit. I'm so tired. I just can't do the nine to five grind anymore."

"Then, what are you going to do?" I asked.

He said, "I just want to go back to buying and fixing houses. Would you consider investing in a property with me?" I told him to come to my office and we'd talk it over. He's a good man and I know his work ethic, so based on that and what I believe about giving back, I agreed to invest in a property with him.

In a way, I was envious of Brian. There is something therapeutic about tearing out walls and hanging sheetrock. It's also nice not having all the headaches that come with having a business—like employees, overhead, obligations, etcetera. Yet, I know that along with those headaches come influence, authority, control and, in this case, the ability to help someone like Brian.

After about a week, Brian found a property that we both knew was a good investment. The house was in fair condition and it was in a nice neighborhood. He came back to my office a few days later, we wrote up a loan contract, and designed a strategy together. He thought he could have the house ready to sell in three months.

True to his word, Brian put the house on the market within the ninety-day window, and it sold about a month later. He provided the deal, I provided the finances, and he provided the labor. It's a perfect example of how The Circle of Wealth works.

At the closing of the sale, I looked over at Brian at the closing table. He was light years away from the broken man he was just months before. His motivation and purpose were reignited again. Because he realized that he could do a deal where we both made money, we started talking about doing it again.

That investment turned into a win-win situation for both Brian and me. More importantly I had used my success and finances to help him. To me, helping people like Brian is the real reason for success.

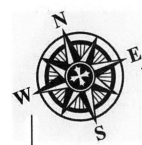

51.4 Degrees of

Completing the Circle

1. How can giving make you more successful?
2. Learn about the true riches in The Circle of Wealth.
3. See the potential in others.
4. See opportunity in helping others.
5. Learn how prayer is the most valuable business tool.
6. Be a good steward of money.

LUKE 19:12-26 (TLB) A nobleman living in a certain province was called away to the distant capital of the empire to be crowned king of his province. Before he left he called together ten assistants and gave them each $2,000 to invest while he was gone. Upon his return he called in the men to whom he had given the money, to find out what they had done with it, and what their profits were.

The first man reported a tremendous gain—ten times as much as the original amount!

"Fine!" the king exclaimed. "You are a good man. You have been faithful with the little I entrusted to you, and as your reward, you shall be governor of ten cities."

The next man also reported a splendid gain—five times the original amount.

"All right!" his master said. "You can be governor over five cities."

But the third man brought back only the money he had started with. "I've kept it safe," he said, "because I was afraid you would demand my profits, for you are a hard man to deal with, taking what isn't yours and even confiscating the crops that others plant."

"You vile and wicked slave", the king roared. "Hard, am I? That's exactly how I'll be toward you! If you knew so much about me and how tough I am, then why didn't you deposit the money in the bank so that I could at least get some interest on it?"

Then turning to the others standing by he ordered, "Take the money away from him and give it to the man who earned the most."

"But, sir," they said, "he has enough already!"

"Yes," the king replied, "but it is always true that those who have, get more, and those who have little, soon lose even that"---

WHAT STEPS ARE YOU GOING TO TAKE TO MAKE A POSITIVE CHANGE?

PART 2
MY VENTURE

I was making money hand-over-fist and feeling and definitely acting rich. I had a million-dollar house, a Range Rover, an Escalade, and a Lexus. I went on expensive vacations and dropped thousands of dollars at dinners and lunches. I basically had a multi-million dollar ego. I was cocky and arrogant. I financed everything I bought and I leveraged everything I owned. I was a Nouveau Riche idiot and I coveted everything I laid my eyes on.

The monthly payment on the Range Rover was $2,300, the Escalade was $1,600, and the Lexus was $860. I was shelling out almost $5,000 a month on just car payments. On top of that, the house payment was $9,600 and we were eating out all the time. It was costing me $30,000 a month just to live. I couldn't walk into a store without dropping thousands of dollars on toys, accessories and "stuff". I loved my life, I loved my stuff, and I had forgotten many of the lessons my parents taught me about being a good steward of my money and my time. I had forgotten many of the Godly lessons that had set me up for this success in the first place. Because of this, God was about to give me a very rude awakening.

When 2008 came, the bottom dropped out of the real estate market. As Warren Buffet said, "It's only when the tide goes out that you learn who has been swimming naked." I was buck naked when the tide went out in 2008 and lost almost everything. It was all I could do to avoid bankruptcy.

I had mentors, but unfortunately, they had nothing to offer me. They were just as young, cocky, and arrogant as I was. The only difference between me and them was that they had more money than I did, and they were able to weather the storm better than I could.

At that time I had a lot of real estate in my portfolio and I had borrowed against all of it to lend out to other investors. When the market crashed, the properties weren't worth even half what I paid for them and the properties I had lent on weren't worth even half of what I had loaned. My little empire came crashing down around me.

I was so leveraged that I had no income that wasn't directly tied to real estate. In 2008, when the tide went out, everything in my financial portfolio went out with it. I remember feeling so beat down and discouraged. I even once asked Jaclyn, "Do you think anyone would hire me?" Suddenly the guy who bragged about never, ever being in a position to work for wages again, was considering a 9-5 job. I was done. Finished. Washed up. Yet Jaclyn was utterly supportive. She encouraged me the entire time and never once suggested that she thought we wouldn't make it.

It was a time of eating huge servings of humble pie. I spent nearly a year calling creditors, sub-contractors, and suppliers to negotiate settlements to keep from going bankrupt. The responses, often sprinkled with words I won't print here, were along the lines of, "What do you mean you can't pay me? I trusted you, Lee. I went out on a limb for you. You said you were a big-deal, real estate investor and you had all kinds of money..."

I was, and I did – until I didn't.

You will have financial challenges on your journey. How you conduct your business leading into them and then how you handle your business after they hit, dictates your rate of success or failure. Customers and creditors will put up with a lot, except being ignored. All you can do is face the problem head on and admit, "I screwed up." Then throw yourself on their mercy and hope for the best.

During this period of time I was hired by Donald Trump's organization to do a mentorship for one of their clients. As I was going to the airport a sudden light and solution began to dawn on me. I had my own mentorship package, which I already knew was a good product and I also had all of my own experiences (both good and bad) that I could offer to my own clients. I could help others enjoy the fruits of their labors without committing the near-fatal errors I had made. When I held an event three weeks later, I offered the mentorship package and we had five sales. That event started to pull us out of the slump, both emotionally and financially.

The real estate crash was incredibly painful on so many levels, but, I learned something I didn't know before that I definitely needed to learn. Unfortunately, I had to learn it the hard way, but truthfully, I was so arrogant at the time, I'm not sure I could have learned it any other way. I learned that I didn't actually own most of what I claimed I owned. I found out that in the end, having a lot of expensive toys, a big beautiful house, and a burgeoning real estate portfolio didn't do me a bit of good, because they could all disappear in a second. In the end, all I had left were my relationships with others, my wife and family, and most importantly my faith in God. The swift kick in the butt put everything back into perspective. God became the center of my life again, and working hard, being diligent about my finances, and becoming a good steward of my business became a core principle in my life.

During this period, my wife and I decided to move from Salt Lake City back to Spokane, Washington. I wanted to raise my family closer to my roots and I also wanted to get away from the mentality I had in Salt Lake City, which was "Anything goes." It was also then that I started my non-profit, non-denominational ministry, *He's the Solution.* Now, each Saturday I send out a Christian email and each Sunday I give a morning Bible-based devotional. Sometimes there are twenty people on the call, sometimes only two, but I mainly preach to stay closer to, and for the glory, of God. I also now always have a church service at all of my events so people who are there to learn about real estate, don't have to miss God's message and neither do I. Since introducing this ministry, my life, my relationships with Jaclyn and the kids, and the health of my business have only gotten better and stronger. It keeps me centered on what's really important.

Now, although I manage millions of dollars, I live in a modest home and Jaclyn and I drive used cars that we paid cash for. There is nothing fancy or flashy about our lives and I'm not leveraged to the hilt. I invest in real estate that I wholesale or fix and flip and only use the cash I've made, or safely borrowed, to invest in new properties. I now have a savings that I don't spend or re-invest. Basically, I've become the unassuming millionaire next door and I'm finally content. When I "thought" I had everything, I wanted more, but now that I *really* have everything—a life centered on God, a wonderful wife and three healthy children, a robust private money company, and a functional real estate investing business, I can honestly say I am sated.

That's not to say I'm done. As Robert Frost said, "I have miles to go before I sleep." I still have many goals and aspirations and I still want my business to grow and be more profitable, but now I know I want them for the right reasons. My business is now built on the principle of helping others reach the same level of success and contentedness that I have. I hope many will be able to say that I helped them in their personal and professional growth and that in one way or another I helped them achieve their dreams.

Jaclyn and my children are everything to me. Before my business crashed I would have told you that, but it wouldn't have been as true as it is today. The best time of day for me is when I pull into my garage and my children come running to meet me. We spend the evening together as a family, eating pizza and watching TV. That's something I never would have done before. It's interesting that by doing what's best for my family, and not striving to make money, I've actually made more money.

I think success is found in a relationship with God. More than anything, it was prayer and my connection to Him that got me through the challenges in the past and keep me going today. Strengthening that relationship is still something I work on. I ultimately want to come to the place, that no matter what's happening in my business or my life, I'm completely reliant on Him, His help, His wisdom, and His guidance.

To me, above all else, that's the true measure of success.

BOOKSHELF

L isted are some of my favorite books that I suggest for interesting reading on your road to wealth.

The Goal: A Process of Ongoing Improvement
by Eliyahu M. Goldratt
Publisher: North River Press
ISBN: 978-0884271956

The Promise of a Pencil: How an Ordinary Person Can Create Extraordinary Change
by Adam Braun
Publisher: Scribner
ISBN: 978-1476730639

People Buy You: The Real Secret to what Matters Most in Business
by Jeb Blount
Publisher: Wiley
ISBN: 978-0470599112

Who Moved My Cheese?: An A-Mazing Way to Deal with Change in Your Work and in Your Life
by Spencer Johnson
Publisher: G. P. Putnam's Sons
ISBN: 978-0399144462

I Moved Your Cheese: For Those Who Refuse to Live as Mice in Someone Else's Maze
by Deepak Malhotra
Publisher: Berrett-Koehler Publishers
ISBN: 978-1609949761

Crossing the Chasm: Marketing and Selling Disruptive Products to Mainstream Customers
by Geoffrey A. Moore
Publisher: HarperBusiness
ISBN: 978-0062292988

The Power of Many: Values for Success in Business and in Life
by Meg Whitman
Publisher: Crown Business
ISBN: 978-0307591227

Life Is a Series of Presentations: Eight Ways to Inspire, Inform, and Influence
by Tony Jeary
Publisher: Touchstone
ISBN: 978-0743269254

The Success System That Never Fails
by William Clement Stone
Publisher: CreateSpace Independent Publishing
ISBN: 978-1492851578

Setting the Table: The Transforming Power of Hospitality in Business
by Danny Meyer
Publisher: Harper Perennial
ISBN: 978-0060742768

Peaks and Valleys: Making Good And Bad Times Work For You– At Work And In Life
by Spencer Johnson M.D.
Publisher: Atria Books
ISBN: 978-1501108082

Brandwashed: Tricks Companies Use to Manipulate Our Minds and Persuade Us to Buy
by Martin Lindstrom
Publisher: Crown Business
ISBN: 978-0385531733

Little Red Book of Selling: 12.5 Principles of Sales Greatness
by Jeffrey Gitomer
Publisher: Bard Press
ISBN: 978-1885167606

Customer Satisfaction Is Worthless, Customer Loyalty Is Priceless
by Jeffery Gitomer
Publisher: Bard Press
ISBN: 978-1885167309

Psycho-Cybernetics, A New Way to Get More Living Out of Life
by Maxwell Maltz
Publisher: Pocket Books
ISBN: 978-0671700751

Coaching Salespeople into Sales Champions: A Tactical Playbook for Managers and Executives
by Keith Rosen
Publisher: Wiley
ISBN: 978-0470142516

The 5 Love Languages: The Secret to Love that Lasts
by Gary D Chapman
Publisher: Northfield Publishing
ISBN: 978-0802412706

LAST CALL

W hen God created man, man fell into sin and needed a Savior. God could make us pay the punishment ourselves or he could send a Messiah which He did in the form of Jesus Christ. Jesus paid the punishment for us so we could be reunited as sons and daughters of God and have eternal salvation in Heaven.

Jesus died and rose again after three days to be the first born among many to escape death of the spirit. He has given us all this free gift. All we have to do is receive that gift. It is ours to take at no price.

Romans 8:2

> *Because through Christ Jesus the law of the Spirit who gives life, has set you free from the law of sin and death. (NIV)*

One of the most amazing things about accepting what Jesus did, is you can't help but feel better. I can tell you from personal experience this is true. I've lived for myself, and I've lived for God. There is a monumental difference.

Fellowship with God is our highest calling. It's not about "earning" your salvation by trying to be good enough. It's not about going to church, taking a vow of poverty, not wearing lipstick, praying to dead saints, or jumping through other man-made hoops. It's about having a relationship with the living God, who wanted to restore that relationship badly enough that He sent His Son as a sacrifice for us.

Just ask God to make Himself real to you and receive a free ticket out of this worldly mess. If you're ready to take the first step, read the following prayer out loud:

> *Heavenly Father, I come to You in the Name of Jesus. I pray and ask Jesus to come into my heart and be Lord over my life. I confess that Jesus is Lord, and I believe in my heart that God raised Him from the dead. Your Word says, "If I confess with my mouth that Jesus is Lord, and believe in my heart that God has raised Him from the dead, I will be saved." I will not fret or have anxiety about anything, Father, for Your peace now guards my heart and soul. You are my source, so I have comfort and encouragement that you will provide everything I need. Thank you for your gift of salvation. I'm a new person in Christ.*

Tell someone about your new faith in Christ. Get baptized in water. Spend some time with God and develop a habit of talking with Him and reading The Bible each day. Ask Him to increase your faith and your understanding of His Word, and find a place where the Word is taught and you can worship freely.

If you said this prayer, and/or need a Bible, email me at: lee@hesthesolution.com with your name and address and I will send you a Bible free, post-paid. Then let me know how it's going with the new and improved you.

Also join me at www.hesthesolution.com for worship, videos, community and our blog.

Or feel free to write or call the ministry any time at:

He's the Solution
1121 E Mullan Ave.
Coeur d'Alene ID 83814
(800) 971-5988

Until we meet again, peace be upon you.

ABOUT THE AUTHOR

LEE A. ARNOLD is the CEO of Secured Investment Corp, The Lee Arnold System of Real Estate Investing, and the rapidly growing private money company, Cogo Capital ©, "The Private Money Company"©.

He grew up in a traditional American family where a college education was taught as the only way to reach financial security. Yet, when his own highly educated father faced a career loss, his family went through a long period of living in financial strain. Lee knew from that moment on he never wanted his income or his future to be left in the hands of someone else.

Lee's desire to reach the heights of financial freedom has allowed him to develop unique investing methods and innovative strategies that he teaches to other real estate investors. Through hard work, in-depth research, and years of full time investing, Lee truly has found the golden key to unlock the door to financial success.

Lee has generated millions of dollars in personal wealth and is known as one of the foremost experts in the foreclosure and short sale industry, as well as the private money market. His goal is to help other investors discover the same success he has found and experience the joy of a truly rewarding career.

Lee conducts free CEO Fireside Chats on the first Monday of every month. These monthly success-building, all-content trainings can help you overcome common obstacles and enhance your business acumen for further growth and development. To join the next one, register at: www.leearnoldsystem.com/ceofireside

If you would like to contact Lee - call (800) 971-5988 or visit www.leearnoldsystem.com. We look forward to getting to know you and helping your business grow.